THE
CANCER SURVIVAL
COOKBOOK

200 Quick & Easy Recipes
with Helpful Eating Hints

Donna L. Weihofen, RD, MS
with Christina Marino, MD, MPH

JOHN WILEY & SONS, INC.

New York • Chichester • Weinheim • Brisbane • Singapore • Toronto

ISBN 0-471-34668-3

Printed in the United States of America

10   9   8   7   6   5

Many thanks to all the special patients in the oncology and radiotherapy clinics at the University of Wisconsin Hospital and Clinics who have given me insight into the fight against cancer. It is your wisdom and practical advice I have used in writing this book. Thank you also to the caring oncology staff and especially to Nancy Joliffe, Phyllis Dearborn, and Judy DeMuth who supported me through the hard days of this project. Thank you to Mary Risgaard who gave me her practical cooking advice and to Christina Marino who gave me her professional cooking advice. Thank you to my husband Ray and my children Wayne, Wendy, and Vicki who put up with me, working endless hours on the computer, in the sunroom. Thank you to Jeff Braun and David Enyeart at Chronimed Publishing who made this book a reality. This book is worth every minute we all put in the project if it will help you win the battle with cancer.

Preface

How often do you think about food? Food not only nourishes your body, it gives pleasure and satisfaction, nourishing your emotions. When you think of a party or celebration, food is a crucial element in the success of the event. But what would happen if you actually lost your appetite and found eating was no longer the pleasure you once remembered? This is often the reality for people with cancer. The medications can make you nauseated, radiation can make your mouth sore, you can lose your taste from the disease or treatments, and the emotional upset from the entire ordeal can reduce your desire to eat. Your family and friends want to be helpful and encourage you to eat because they know it will help you recover faster. It can be hard for someone to even comprehend how difficult it is to eat when you are being treated for cancer.

That's why we wrote this book. I was treated for cancer twice. Both times were filled with battles with food and I lost the battle frequently after chemotherapy sessions, not being able to swallow, not finding any pleasure in the taste of food, finding the smell of food cooking extremely nauseating and to this day, not being able to think about certain foods because I vomited these foods after chemotherapy sessions! I struggled to keep weight on during radiation therapy treatments for Hodgkin's lymphoma. I was reluctant to ask for help because I should have known the answers to these problems. I was a physician.

You do not have to go through the same ordeal. This book is full of eating hints to help you overcome many of the problems encountered during cancer therapy. If you can eat, you can help your body recover from cancer and the treatments necessary to eradicate the disease. This is not a book filled with bizarre advice on unproven, expensive nutrients and supplements. It is filled with comfort foods and professional cooking hints. Professional? Sure, because I also have been trained in the culinary arts. And if you think that is not enough professional advice, the main author is a nutritionist who specializes in working with

PREFACE

cancer patients. Most of these recipes are written with nutrition and delicious taste in mind and therefore are great for the whole family, but also many of the recipes have a high-calorie modification if you need extra calories. We have tried to include recipes that are everybody's favorites and recipes that require minimal preparation time and effort; we've also added some of the new varieties of foods that are popular in our culture. You may even find cooking therapeutic as you create great tasting meals. You do not have to exist on baby food or bland crackers when you are going through chemotherapy or radiation therapy. This book can be your companion to making the treatment of and recovery from cancer manageable. Use it and enjoy the pleasure, comfort, and healing power of eating.

Christina Marino

Table of Contents

Introduction

The joy of eating good food enhances the quality of our lives. This book of tasty recipes and eating tips will provide you and your family with good food and good nutrition. Eating well will help in fighting the battle against cancer.

There are lots of recipes using fruits and vegetables. If there is any magic to preventing and fighting cancer with nutrition, it is most likely in eating more fruits and vegetables. It is important to emphasize there is no single food that will cure cancer, but there are nutrients and phytochemicals in foods that will help you in the fight.

The majority of recipes are easy to make; some take a little extra time in preparation, but they're worth the effort. Since most people today have limited time or energy to spend cooking, this is not a complicated gourmet cookbook. Most of the recipes use common ingredients—ones you probably keep on hand in your kitchen.

Many of the recipes are healthy and low in fat. The recipes are tasty creations that you will enjoy, along with your family and friends. There are also some recipes that are great if you have special needs for moist, softer foods. There may be times when you are interested in higher calorie recipes if you have problems with weight loss. Since you may not have had to deal with weight loss problems before, there are many recipes that have notations to guide you in increasing the calories. Some foods are concentrated in calories to help you maintain your weight if your appetite is poor. There is a nutrition analysis of every recipe to help you make appropriate recipe choices.

Special Features of the Book Include:

Eating Hints

There is a comprehensive section on "Eating Hints" for problems you may encounter during chemotherapy or radiotherapy. What do you do if your appetite just isn't up to par, you're not hungry, or you fill up too fast? This section is full of ideas that have worked for others. Many of the recommendations have come from the hundreds of cancer patients I've worked with at the University of Wisconsin Comprehensive Cancer Center.

Snacking Section

The section on "Snacking" will help you when you can't eat enough with just three meals a day. There are times when you may benefit from becoming a nibbler or a grazer. By eating small amounts frequently, you may be able to maintain your weight better.

Herbal Remedies

In light of the growing interest in using herbs to try to improve health, we present a comprehensive discussion on herbal remedies—those known to be harmful and those that have promising benefits.

Other Unique Features

Easy Lunches. Quick meals for those times when you want good home-cooked food but don't have the time or energy to prepare much at all.

Beverage Section. Ideas for beverages when you need extra calories or you have to drink lots of extra fluid.

Main Course Sections. Emphasis on chicken, eggs, and vegetables for times when red meat is not so appealing.

Dessert Section. Some traditional sweet desserts but also some ideas for times when sweets just do not appeal to you.

Soft and Pureed Section. Ideas for pureed foods.

Fiber Foods. New information on the fiber content of food will be invaluable for the times you may need either high-fiber or low-fiber foods.

Lists of Potassium-Rich and Magnesium-Rich Foods. Some medications and chemotherapy cause potassium and magnesium deficiency.

INTRODUCTION

Neutropenic Diet Recommendations. Neutrophils are one type of white blood cell that fight infections. A low neutrophil count is called neutropenia. Some adjustments are needed in your diet when you are neutropenic to prevent food-borne illness.

Eating Hints to Fight Cancer

Eating Hints

Eating can be a fun, pleasant part of your life or it can become hard and
frustrating. If you are dealing with cancer, you may be confused by the
conflicting advice you get from the media or even from family and
friends. You have heard about the foods to eat or not to eat to prevent
cancer. But now what? You have cancer.

The diet that is promoted to prevent cancer, such as a low-fat, high-
fiber diet, may not be the diet that is needed during certain periods of
cancer treatment. This is the time to switch gears and deal with the
problems of today. This is the time to nourish your body with all the
nutrients you need to stay strong and fight this disease. The number one
nutrient needed now is calories, and a major source of concentrated
calories is fats. Calories and fats have a bad name. In fact, you may have
spent most of your life trying to limit or avoid them. You will need to
make peace with them now. They are crucial if you have a waning
appetite or you have other problems that affect your eating. Fruits and
vegetables are still very important, but perhaps they need to be served
with high-calorie, high-protein sauces.

There is no evidence that any special diet or any single food will cure
cancer or prevent it from recurring. On the other hand, certain uncon-
ventional diets may be harmful. These diets do not include an adequate
variety of foods and are deficient in essential nutrients, including protein, fats, and calories. The jury is still out as to the necessity for using
dietary supplements, including taking higher doses than normally recommended of vitamin and mineral pills, to cure cancer. There is evidence that too much of some supplements can actually be harmful or
interfere with chemotherapy treatments. Check with your physician,
dietitian, or nurse before taking any type of vitamin, mineral, or dietary
supplement.

Anorexia, the loss of appetite or desire to eat, is the most common
symptom that causes trouble for those who have cancer. It may occur
even before you know you have cancer, during the treatment, or when

the disease has spread. Anorexia causes decreased food intake, which triggers malnutrition and the loss of muscle strength. When your body does not get enough protein, calories, and other nutrients, it affects how well you fight infections and how well your body is able to fight your cancer. Your nutritional health has a direct effect on how well and how long you can battle cancer.

There are many reasons for anorexia. It can be due to the cancer itself, the treatments you are getting, or the stress of coping with the cancer diagnosis. You may feel a loss of control over your life, but in the area of food and eating, you can regain some control. You can decide to eat even though you don't feel like eating, you aren't very hungry, the food tastes different, or the smell of food bothers you. You can decide to eat to keep your strength and you can decide to let friends and family cater to you a little.

There is help for you if you have problems with eating. There are new drugs that increase the appetite and control or decrease nausea and vomiting. Practical and helpful information has also been gathered from other patients and from experienced health professionals to provide you with eating hints for specific problems in the next sections.

4

"I'm not hungry."

Loss of appetite or anorexia is a common problem. Sometimes treatments such as radiation or chemotherapy are the cause, but it also happens at times to people who are not having treatments. It may be related to changes in metabolism during cancer, pain, fatigue, stress, depression, or a combination of all of these factors. Appetite can come and go. You may be just temporarily not interested in eating. Try to take advantage of times when food tastes good and eat to your maximum.

General Suggestions

Eat small amounts of appealing foods frequently throughout the day. Become a grazer. Do not expect to eat regular size meals.

It may help you to eat by the clock. Set the clock for every 2 to 4 hours and eat a small snack even if you are not hungry.

Keep snacks handy for nibbling. Make it easy to snack at any time. Carry a snack pack of easy-to-eat nibbles in your pocket or purse. Ideas for your snack pack include granola, nuts, pretzels, dried fruit, crackers with cheese or peanut butter, bite-size candy, or homemade trail mix.

Eat foods you really like during periods when you aren't very hungry.

Eat a snack before going to bed in addition to other meals.

Weigh yourself every three or four days to make sure your weight remains stable.

If you begin losing weight, refer to the section on Hints to Increase Calories starting on page 6.

Dealing With Meal Time

Select foods that remind you of happy times. Most of us have special comfort foods that cheer us up, like mashed potatoes or meat loaf. Select those foods frequently. Some patients find they can eat more if they choose foods they liked as children.

Increase or decrease the seasonings and flavorings of your food to accommodate any taste changes you may be experiencing.

Try to make meal time enjoyable with an attractive setting and colorful, tasty foods.

Drink a glass of wine or beer before meals. This often stimulates the appetite. (Check with your physician to make sure small amounts of alcohol are OK.)

Use a plate that is larger than needed and put small portions on the plate. That way the amount of food that you need to eat does not look so overwhelming!

Try changing the time, place, and surroundings of meals. Eat with others or watch your favorite TV program while you eat.

Create a mealtime atmosphere that is relaxed and unhurried.

If this is a time when you really do not enjoy eating, you may want to concentrate on eating and drinking just for the nutritional value of the food. One patient stated, "My body doesn't care if food tastes good or bad and it doesn't care if I don't feel like eating, but my body does need nutrition to fight the cancer."

"I feel so full after eating just a little."

There may be times when you seem to fill up fast even though you used to be a big eater. It is important to maintain your weight by choosing high-calorie foods and foods that are rich in nutrients.

General Suggestions

Eat only foods that are rich in calories and nutrients. Avoid low-calorie foods that fill you up, such as lettuce, broth, and diet soda.

When choosing beverages, select nutrient-dense fluids such as milk, milk shakes, juice and punch-type drinks.

5

Limit the amount of fluids you drink with your meals. Liquids tend to make you feel full. Save the water, tea, coffee, and other liquids for between meals.

Place small servings of food on your plate so it does not seem to be such an impossible task to eat a whole meal. Cut sandwiches into smaller pieces.

Keep ready-to-eat snack foods readily available, and even at your bedside in case you wake up during the night. Ideas include pretzels, nuts, crackers, cookies, dried fruits, granola bars, and rice cakes.

Eat small amounts of food frequently.

6

Hints to Increase Calories
(*denotes foods high in both calories and protein)

Nuts and Peanut Butter*
1/4 cup nuts = 200 calories
2 Tbsp. peanut butter = 200 calories

❖ Add nuts to cookies, muffins, and breads.
❖ Sprinkle nuts on vegetables and salads.
❖ Snack on nuts.
❖ Spread peanut butter on fruits such as apples and bananas.
❖ Spread peanut butter on crackers.

Granola*
1 1/2 oz. = about 200 calories

❖ Sprinkle on vegetables, yogurt, ice cream, pudding, and fruits.
❖ Mix with nuts and dried fruits for snacks.

Dried fruits
3 oz. dried apricots = 200 calories
10 pitted prunes = 200 calories
1/3 cup raisins = 200 calories
1/2 cup dried cranberries = 200 calories
7 pitted dates = 200 calories
4 mission figs = 200 calories

❖ Cook and serve for meals or snacks.
❖ Add to muffins, cookies, breads, rice, grain dishes, cereals, puddings, and stuffing.
❖ Combine with cooked vegetables, such as carrots, sweet potatoes, and squash.
❖ Combine with nuts or granola for snacks.

Eggs*
1 cup chopped cooked egg = 200 calories
2 1/2 whole eggs = 200 calories

❖ It is not safe to eat raw or undercooked eggs.
❖ Add chopped, hard-cooked eggs to salads and dressings, vegetables, casseroles, and creamed meats.
❖ Beat eggs into mashed potatoes, sweet potatoes, vegetable purees, and sauces. Be sure to cook these dishes after adding the eggs.
❖ Add extra eggs to quiche, custard, pudding, pancakes, or French toast.
❖ Make a rich custard with eggs, milk, and sugar.

7

Honey, Jam, and Sugar
3 Tbsp. honey = 200 calories
4 Tbsp. jam = 200 calories
4 1/2 Tbsp. sugar = 200 calories

❖ Spread jam or honey on bread, bagels, and toast. Add honey to cereal, milk drinks, yogurt, ice cream, and desserts.
❖ Use whipped or creamed flavored honey as a spread.
❖ Use honey or jam as a glaze for meats such as chicken or ham.
❖ Use extra sugar or honey to sweeten foods and drinks.
❖ Drizzle honey over biscuits and other breads.

Salad Dressing and Mayonnaise
2 Tbsp. regular mayonnaise or regular dressing = 200 calories

❖ Choose regular dressings and mayonnaise instead of reduced-fat dressings.
❖ Spread on sandwiches and crackers.
❖ Combine with meat, fish, egg, pasta, rice, or vegetable salads.
❖ Use in fruit salads.
❖ Use in cold dipping sauces and gelatin dishes.

Sour Cream
1/3 cup or 6 Tbsp. = 200 calories

❖ Add to cream soups, potatoes, noodle dishes, vegetables, sauces, salad dressings, stews, cooked meats, and fish.
❖ Use as a sauce on cooked meats.
❖ Use as a topping for cakes, fruit, gelatin desserts, breads, and muffins.

"I FEEL SO FULL..."

❖ Use as a dip for fresh fruits and vegetables.
❖ Add to brown sugar and mix with fruits.

Cream Cheese
2 oz. or 4 Tbsp. = 200 calories

❖ Spread on breads, crackers, muffins, bagels, and fruit slices.
❖ Use in vegetable dips.
❖ Roll into balls and coat with chopped nuts, wheat germ, or granola for snacks.
❖ Whip into mashed potatoes and other vegetables.

Table Cream
10 Tbsp. half & half = 200 calories
6 1/2 Tbsp. light = 200 calories
5 1/2 Tbsp. medium = 200 calories

❖ Use in coffee, cream soups, sauces, egg dishes, batters, pudding, and custard.
❖ Pour on hot or cold cereal and over fruits.
❖ Mix with pasta, rice, and mashed potatoes.
❖ Pour on chicken and fish while baking.
❖ Use as a binder in ground meats.
❖ Use in place of part of the milk in recipes.
❖ Make hot chocolate with cream and add marshmallows.

Heavy Cream
1/4 cup or 4 Tbsp. unwhipped heavy cream = 200 calories
3/4 cup whipped cream = about 200 calories

❖ Use sweetened whipped cream on hot chocolate, desserts, gelatin, pudding, fruit, pancakes, and waffles.
❖ Fold unsweetened heavy cream into mashed potatoes or other mashed vegetables.

Butter or Margarine
2 Tbsp. butter or regular margarine = 200 calories

❖ Add extra amount to potatoes and other cooked vegetables.
❖ Use as a melted dip for seafood, fish, meat, and vegetables.
❖ Add to soup and gravy.
❖ Add extra amount to pasta, rice, hot cereal, grits, and popcorn.
❖ Combine with herbs and seasonings and spread on cooked meat, hamburgers, fish, and egg dishes.

❖ Spread on bread while it is still warm so more will melt into the bread.

Ice Cream
Ice cream varies from 150 to 350 calories per 1/2-cup serving.

❖ Use in beverages such as milk shakes and floats.

❖ Eat as a snack.

❖ Top cereal, fruit, and desserts with ice cream.

❖ Make ice cream sandwiches with cookies or graham crackers.

Creamers, non-dairy
about 1/3 cup powdered = 200 calories
about 3/4 cup liquid = 200 calories

❖ Add to soup, gravy, sauce, hot cereal, and milk shakes.

❖ Use flavored creamers in coffee.

Glucose Polymers
Polycose or Sumacal = 23 calories per tablespoon

❖ Commercial glucose polymers can be added to foods to increase calories without adding extra sweetness. They contain fewer calories than the same amount of fat but they may be helpful to use when you do not want the richness of fat. They do not add any flavor or texture to the food.

❖ Add powder or liquid form to cooked vegetables, casseroles, stews, desserts, and beverages.

Commercial Supplements*
1 cup – 240 to 600 calories depending upon the product selected

❖ Drink high-calorie nutritional supplements as needed to help maintain or improve nutritional status.

Food Preparation Hints
❖ Bread meats and vegetables.

❖ Fry or sauté meats and vegetables.

❖ Be generous with the amount of sauce or gravy added to pasta, vegetables, and meat.

❖ Choose creamed, buttered, and au gratin recipes.

Adapted from National Institutes of Health Publication No. 94-2079

Hints to Increase Protein
Protein is essential for maintaining your muscle and lean body mass. It is also essential to enhance your immune system. The normal requirement for protein is about 50 to 75 grams per day. With cancer it may

be beneficial to increase protein to 80 to 90 grams per day. You do not have to count the grams of protein you eat each day, but if you want to estimate your intake, you can count the grams in a typical day.

1 ounce meat, poultry, or fish = 7 grams
1 serving lentils, dry beans, or peas (1/2 cup) = 6 grams
1 cup milk (whole, 2%, 1%, skim) = 8 grams
1 ounce cheese = 6 grams
1 serving bread products (1 slice) = 2 grams
1 serving pasta or rice (1/2 cup) = 2 grams

The following foods provide significant amounts of protein.

Cheese

2 oz. regular cheese = 200 calories & 12 gm. protein
2 oz. reduced-fat cheese = 100–180 calories & 12 gm. protein
2 oz. fat-free cheese = 45 calories & 8 gm. protein

❖ Grate and add to mashed potatoes, other cooked vegetables, casseroles, pasta, rice, and sauces.

❖ Melt on bread or bagels under the broiler.

❖ Melt on hamburgers, hot dogs, brats, and sandwiches.

❖ Use as a snack with crackers.

❖ Serve with apple pie or other fruit desserts.

Cottage Cheese and Ricotta Cheese

1 cup 4% cottage cheese = 240 calories & 28 gm. protein
1 cup low-fat cottage cheese = 160–200 calories & 28 gm. protein
1 cup ricotta = 430 calories & 30 gm. protein
1 cup part-skim ricotta = 350 calories & 30 gm. protein
1 cup nonfat ricotta = 210 calories & 30 gm. protein

❖ Add to pasta dishes, casseroles, quiche, and egg dishes.

❖ Use in desserts such as gelatin and cheesecakes.

Eggs

2 1/2 whole eggs = 200 calories & 17 gm. protein
1 cup chopped cooked egg = 200 calories & 17 gm. protein

❖ It is not safe to eat raw or undercooked eggs.

❖ Add extra eggs to batters for French toast, pancakes, waffles, and quiche.

❖ Beat into mashed potatoes, vegetable purees, and sauces. Be sure to cook these dishes after adding the eggs.

❖ Add hard-cooked eggs to casseroles, creamed meats, salads, and vegetable dishes.

❖ Add eggs to casseroles and pasta dishes.

❖ Select recipes that use eggs, such as bread pudding, rice pudding, custard, and other cooked puddings.

Instant Breakfast Powders

❖ Add to any milk-based beverage or food such as cocoa, milk shakes, and instant pudding.

❖ Drink between meals.

Legumes—Dried Beans, Peas, and Lentils
1 cup = about 200 calories and 12 gm. protein

❖ Mash cooked or canned legumes for dips or spreads.

❖ Mix cooked or canned beans in salads, casseroles, pasta, or rice dishes.

❖ Serve as a main course salad.

Meat, Fish, and Poultry
3 oz. = about 200 calories and 20 gm. protein

❖ Add extra cooked chopped meats to casseroles, stew, pasta, salad, soup, stuffing, omelets, and potatoes and other vegetables.

❖ Add cooked cubes of meat or seafood to sauces and serve over pasta, rice, bread, or biscuits.

Milk
1 cup whole milk = 160 calories & 8 gm. protein
1 cup 2% milk = 120 calories & 8 gm. protein
1 cup 1% milk = 100 calories & 8 gm. protein
1 cup skim milk = 90 calories & 8 gm. protein

❖ Use milk in recipes that require water such as instant cocoa, soup, bread or muffin mixes, hot cereal mixes, or pancake mixes. (Note: It does not work well to cook rice or pasta in milk.)

❖ Add to hot cereal, hot chocolate, pudding, sauces, and soup.

Fortified Milk—Double Protein Milk
1 cup made with whole milk = 275 calories & 14 gm. protein
1 cup made with 1% milk = 200 calories & 14 gm. protein

❖ **Fortified milk recipe:** Mix 1 quart whole milk or 1 quart low-fat milk with 1 cup instant nonfat milk powder. Refrigerate at least 4 hours before drinking for better flavor.

❖ Use as milk in recipes that call for water or milk, such as soup, cereal, cocoa, pudding, casseroles, and desserts.

11

Powdered Milk

1/3 cup nonfat dry milk powder = 80 calories & 8 gm. protein

❖ Add to many foods such as cooked cereal, ground meat, casseroles, creamed or mashed potatoes, sauce, gravy, soup, pudding, custard, bread batter, dessert batter, pancake batter, and milk beverages.

Buttermilk

1 cup buttermilk = 110 calories & 9 gm. protein

❖ Use in pancake or waffle mixes.

❖ Use in place of milk in mashed potatoes for a tart taste.

❖ Use in place of sour cream as a topping for baked potatoes.

❖ Mix with mayonnaise and fresh herbs to make salad dressing.

Nuts and Peanut Butter

1/4 cup nuts = 200 calories & 9 gm. protein
2 Tbsp. peanut butter = 200 calories & 7 gm. protein

❖ Add nuts to cookies, muffins, pancakes, waffles, cereal, and bread.

❖ Sprinkle nuts on vegetables, salads, ice cream, yogurt, and desserts.

❖ Snack on nuts.

❖ Spread peanut butter on fruits such as apples and bananas. Spread on celery sticks.

❖ Spread peanut butter on crackers, muffins, bread, and bagels.

❖ Add peanut butter to frosting.

Wheat Germ

1 oz. = 100 calories & 8 gm. protein

❖ Use as a crunchy topping for casseroles, vegetables, cereal, yogurt, and ice cream.

❖ Add to batters for pancakes, waffles, French toast, muffins, and bread.

❖ Substitute in any recipe that calls for bread crumbs.

Yogurt

1 cup = 80–150 calories & 8–12 gm. protein (check label)

❖ Eat as a snack.

❖ Add to fruit and vegetable dishes.

❖ Use as a dip for fruits, vegetables, or chips.

❖ Use as a topping for baked potatoes instead of sour cream.

❖ Add to dressings for salads or fruits; add to sauces.

❖ **Prepare yogurt cheese:** Spoon yogurt into a paper coffee filter, and place over a small bowl or glass. Refrigerate for several hours or overnight. Discard the liquid whey. Use thickened yogurt for dips or to replace sour cream in some recipes. (See also page 52.)

Adapted from National Institutes of Health Publication No. 94-2079

"I get tired easily. I don't have much energy."

When you are being treated for cancer with chemotherapy or radio-therapy, fatigue can become a life-disrupting problem. Fatigue may be experienced as tiredness, weakness, lack of energy, or sheer exhaustion. Learning to recognize and respect your limits often means making adjustments in exercise, work, sleep, eating, and social schedules. Getting extra rest is important and so is eating plenty of nutritious food, because inadequate intake of calories and other nutrients can compound fatigue. Adjusting eating schedules and food choices can help.

13

General Suggestions

Eat as much as possible at your best time of day. If fatigue worsens later in the day, eat a larger breakfast or lunch.

You may feel more like eating after you have napped or rested.

Eat many small meals and snacks throughout the day.

Avoid skipping meals and snacks. Choose liquid nutritional supplements to replace a meal or snack if easy-to-prepare food is unavailable.

At times when you have more energy, prepare foods in quantity. Refrigerate or freeze them for eating later.

Keep leftovers in single-serving containers so they can be easily warmed in the microwave.

Use frozen or canned convenience foods that require little preparation.

Purchase supermarket deli foods and carryout food from restaurants.

Accept the offers of family and friends to help out.

Check on availability of "Meals on Wheels" in your community.

Check on the availability of a "Take Out Taxi" service in your area. These services will pick up foods from participating restaurants and deliver them to your door.

"I have problems with nausea and vomiting."

Nausea and vomiting are often temporary conditions related to the treatments you are receiving. There are new and better drugs available that can help relieve these side effects. In addition, relaxation methods such as tension reduction, deep rhythmic breathing, quiet concentration, imagery, distractions, biofeedback, and hypnosis have helped many people with cancer cope with the stress and discomfort associated with cancer and its treatments.

General Suggestions

14

Ask your doctor or pharmacist to help you find the most effective medication regimen to prevent or control nausea and vomiting. The medications are more effective if taken before symptoms occur.

Eat small amounts of food throughout the day. Eat before you get hungry. If you get too hungry, feelings of nausea are intensified.

Your tastes will change from hour to hour and day to day. What appeals to you at one time may not appeal to you at another time.

Choose foods that are served cold or at room temperature.

Eat mildly seasoned foods; avoid fatty or greasy foods.

Eat dry foods such as dry cereal, toast, or crackers without liquids, especially when you get up in the morning.

Avoid all cooking odors and foods with strong odors. You may want to try colorless and odorless foods such as cottage cheese, cream soup, white potatoes, macaroni and cheese, applesauce, gelatin, plain rice, sugared rice, rice pudding, and vanilla ice cream. Other suggestions include sherbet, gelatin, sorbet, pretzels, cereal, canned fruit, yogurt, or whatever appeals to you at the time.

Avoid drinking liquids with at meals. Drink or sip liquids slowly between meals and snacks. Try hot tea with honey. Ginger tea may help reduce nausea.

Clear, cool beverages are often well tolerated, but choose whatever liquids you feel you can handle.

Sip liquids slowly through a straw from a covered cup or can. It may be tolerated better if you do not have to smell it.

Eat and drink slowly and try to relax.

Do not eat your favorite foods during this period of time. The foods will no longer be favorite foods if you begin to associate them with nausea and vomiting episodes.

After eating, rest by sitting up or reclining with your head elevated. Keep your head at least four inches higher than your feet. Do not lie down flat for at least two hours after eating. Exercising after eating may slow down digestion and increase your discomfort.

Fresh air and loose clothing may be helpful after eating. Sit near a window where you can watch activities to keep you distracted.

Avoid loud noise and unnecessary conversations when you are nauseated. The effort of talking makes the nausea worse.

Listen to music through headphones. Listen to a tape of a novel being read. Let yourself become involved in the music or book to keep your mind off the nausea.

Try breathing through your mouth when you feel nauseated.

Remove dentures or partial dentures if you are very nauseated since objects in the mouth often tend to promote vomiting.

If your nausea is persistent, keep track of when your nausea occurs and what makes it worse (specific foods, events, surroundings, time of day, etc.). Work with your nutritionist or other health professionals to find solutions.

Check with your physician if you have the following symptoms:
 * ❖ feel bloated
 * ❖ have pain or a swollen stomach before nausea and vomiting occurs
 * ❖ you vomit every time after eating

Replenish lost fluids with clear liquids such as broth, juice, soda, sports drinks, or water. Use electrolyte replacement fluids if vomiting is persistent. Once you have controlled vomiting, try small amounts of clear liquids. Begin with a tablespoon every 5 minutes, gradually increasing the amount to 1/4 cup every 15 minutes. When you are able to keep down clear liquids, try a full liquid diet, gradually working up to your regular diet. (Any food that is liquid at room temperature is considered a full liquid.)

"I can't even stand the smell of food."

General Suggestions

Let someone else do the cooking.

Have food prepared outside your living area. If smells such as brewing coffee bother you, try putting cooking appliances in the porch or garage, if it can be done safely.

Use prepared frozen foods that can be warmed in a microwave.

Choose foods that do not need to be cooked, such as a cold sandwich, yogurt, cottage cheese, pasta salad, and cheese.

Order deli foods or other precooked meals.

Do not fry foods or cook aromatic foods such as pot roast.

Avoid eating in a room that is stuffy, too warm, or has cooking odors or smells that disagree with you.

"Food just doesn't taste the same."

Chemotherapy, radiation therapy, or the cancer itself may cause this problem. Some people have a bitter or a metallic taste in their mouth. For others, food tastes "like nothing." People frequently say they no longer enjoy red meat. For others, the desire for sweets is gone. Taste preferences can change from day to day.

General Suggestions

Many foods, including meat and poultry, taste better if they are served cold or at room temperature instead of hot.

Eggs often taste good when the taste for meat is lost.

Fresh fruits and vegetables, pasta dishes, and milk products are often well tolerated.

Fruit sorbet, sherbet, and fruit smoothies usually taste good.

Tart foods with more distinctive tastes may be added to foods to help cover the metallic taste. Try adding orange, lime, or lemon juice or orange marmalade to fruit salad, salsa, sauces for pork or chicken, stir-fried or cooked vegetables, and oil-based salad dressing. Add vinegar, lemon juice, or pickles to creamy dressings for potato, macaroni, tuna, egg, or cole slaw salads. Lemon juice added to chicken broth, broth-based soup, gazpacho, or guacamole enhances the flavor.

Peel carrots before eating or cooking. This eliminates the bitterness that is quite noticeable to some people and makes them avoid eating carrots altogether. Try the "baby" carrots available in the produce section that are already peeled and cut.

If you do not have sores in your mouth, try using horseradish or any of the flavored mustards, such as Dijon, honey, sweet and sour, etc., to add flavor to your sandwiches and other foods.

Fruit juice popsicles often taste good. Make your own popsicles with your favorite juice flavors.

Rinse your mouth with fruit juice, wine, tea, ginger ale, club soda, or salted water before eating. This will help clear your taste buds.

You can sometimes get rid of the strange taste in your mouth by eating foods that leave their own taste in your mouth, such as fresh fruit or hard candy

17

Suck on lemon drops or mints or chew gum after eating to get rid of undesirable tastes that linger.

Try marinating meat or poultry in fruit juice, wine, vinegar-based salad dressing, or other sauces for more taste.

Experiment with spices and herbs. Some people find they like spicier foods at this time.

Experiment with new foods. Try foods or cuisines you may not have tried before.

Eat out in restaurants that feature buffets. You can try small amounts of a variety of food without having to prepare it yourself.

Check with your dentist to rule out dental problems causing bad taste. Care for your mouth and teeth to prevent dental caries.

Things to Avoid

Do not force yourself to eat foods that taste bad. Instead, find substitutes for those foods. For example, if red meat doesn't taste right, select chicken, turkey, fish, eggs, cottage cheese, cheese, yogurt, or tofu.

Avoid eating no-salt-added or low-salt varieties of canned soups or vegetables (unless you have high blood pressure and are instructed to do so by your physician). Soup and vegetables tend to have a metallic taste when the salt is eliminated in the processing.

Do not drink citrus juices such as orange or grapefruit immediately after brushing your teeth with fluoride toothpaste. The chemical mixture of fluoride with citric acid makes a rather unpleasant taste in your mouth.

If a metallic taste in your mouth persists, avoid using metal dishes and utensils. Try using plastic eating utensils, chopsticks, or porcelain Chinese soup spoons.

Avoid metal cooking utensils. Use plastic or Teflon cooking utensils, wooden spoons, and rubber spatulas.

Avoid cooking with shiny, thin aluminum cookware, copper cookware, or cast iron frying pans or pots. Some of the metal may transfer to the food, especially if the food is acidic. Choose stainless steel or glass cookware.

Smoking cigarettes and drinking alcoholic beverages blunt and distort your ability to taste. Alcohol also makes your mouth dry.

"My mouth is extremely dry."

Radiation therapy and some types of chemotherapy affect the salivary glands and may cause a dry mouth and painful swelling of the glands. There may be a decrease of saliva. The resulting saliva may become very thick, sticky, and stringy. Saliva is one of those things you do not appreciate until it is gone. Saliva moistens the mouth, and that moisture helps you talk, eat, swallow, and keep your teeth and gums healthy. When your body fails to produce enough saliva, the condition is called xerostomia or, more commonly, dry mouth. This may be a temporary problem, although in some cases it is a permanent condition.

General Suggestions

Ask your doctor to recommend a mouth-coating spray or wetting agent to moisten your dry mouth. You can also make your own mouth lubricant with a mixture of 1/4 teaspoon of glycerin added to 1 cup of water.

Chew sugarless gum or suck on sugar-free candy to stimulate saliva. The citrus-flavored candies such as lemon drops work best.

Carry a squirt bottle or water bottle so you'll always have water at hand. Keep water by your bed for night dryness.

Rinse your mouth with a baking soda solution before and after meals. Mix 1/4 teaspoon of baking soda in 1 cup of water. Do not drink the solution.

Dealing with dry mouth at meal time and snack time

Make stews, casseroles, and simmered foods, adding more liquids to make them softer.

Moisten food with sauce, gravy, yogurt, or salad dressing.

Dip or soak food in whatever you are drinking.

Soften or thin food with milk, broth, water, or melted margarine.

Chop, grind, or puree food. A portable food grinder may be helpful.

"MY MOUTH IS EXTREMELY DRY."

Sip drinks often while eating. Use a straw if it helps you swallow.

Choose fruits and juices that are low in acid, such as bananas, apples, or canned fruits. Fruit nectar and fruit drinks may be better tolerated than fruit juices.

Suck on fruit juice popsicles, ice chips, or other cold foods. Cold foods can be soothing.

Keep small pieces of fruit in the freezer and suck or chew on the frozen fruit between meals. Fruits that work well include blueberries, banana pieces, melon balls, peach slices, cherries, fruit cocktail, and mandarin oranges, and grapes.

Choose smooth, soft, creamy foods like soup, macaroni and cheese, mashed potatoes, casseroles, canned fruit, tender cooked vegetables, pudding, custard, and ice cream.

19

Vary the flavor of pureed and soft foods as tolerated to minimize taste fatigue.

Drink cold high-calorie liquids such as milk shakes, instant breakfast drinks, and liquid nutritional supplements. They provide calories and nutrients and are easy to eat.

Use viscous lidocaine or analgesics before meals.

Consider tube feedings if oral intake does not meet your nutritional needs.

Things to Avoid

Avoid peanut butter on crackers, toast, or bread. If you love peanut butter, mix it with lots of honey, jam, or jelly.

Avoid hard, crunchy foods such as tough or crisp meats and dry snack foods.

Avoid foods that gum up in your mouth, such as bread products.

Avoid spicy, salty, or acidic foods that can irritate your mouth.

Avoid pickles and garden vegetables marinated in vinegar.

Avoid hot foods and beverages. Room temperature foods are recommended.

Avoid caffeinated or highly sugared drinks. Drinks with caffeine may cause added dryness.

Avoid alcohol and tobacco. Tobacco can irritate the lining of your mouth and alcohol can make dry mouth worse.

Avoid commercial mouthwashes that contain alcohol. They can dry and irritate your mouth.

Dental Care

Rinse your mouth whenever you feel you need to remove debris, stimulate your gums, lubricate your mouth, or put a fresh taste in your mouth.

Try artificial saliva.

Avoid frequent intake of high sugar foods, which promote tooth decay.

Clean your mouth and teeth often, using a method recommended by your dentist.

Visit your dentist often. With a dry mouth, you are at greater risk of infection, tooth decay, and more rapid plaque buildup.

20

"My mouth and throat are so sore."

The linings of the mouth and throat are among the most sensitive areas of the body and may be quite sensitive to some types of chemotherapy and to radiation treatments. The mouth and throat may become very sore. Healing will occur more rapidly if you eat well and drink ample fluids.

General Suggestions

Make your foods softer and moister.

Chop foods or puree them in the blender. The consistency will change, but not the flavor. Try pureeing

❖ meat to add to soup, mashed potatoes, or gravy.

❖ fruit to add to milk or yogurt.

❖ vegetables to add to soup.

❖ pasta or casseroles.

❖ cottage cheese and fruit.

❖ a piece of pie with a scoop of ice cream.

❖ ice cubes with fruit to make an icy slush.

Foods that are often well tolerated include: pudding, custard, tapioca, applesauce, cream of wheat, pureed room temperature soup, mashed potatoes, mashed sweet potatoes, and scrambled eggs.

Add seasonings to commercial baby foods.

Moisten dry foods in liquids: dip crackers in soup, toast in cocoa, and cookies in milk.

Add sauces such as margarine, butter, gravy, cheese sauce, and cream sauce to your meat and vegetables.

Eat or drink cool foods or beverages, which tend to be soothing.

Keep small pieces of fruit in the freezer and suck or chew on the frozen fruit between meals. Fruits that work well include blueberries, banana pieces, melon balls, peach slices, cherries, fruit cocktail, and mandarin oranges. The cold fruits may be soothing to sores in the mouth.

Try using a straw.

Eat in restaurants that feature buffets where there are a variety of foods you can try in small quantities. You can add sauces and liquids to the food at your discretion. Some patients recommend that you dine during the off-hours when there are not many other customers.

Make a soothing, effective mouth rinse with 1 teaspoon of baking soda in 1 cup of warm water. Avoid mouthwash products that contain a large amount of salt, alcohol, or other irritating ingredients.

21

Some patients report that holding a wet tea bag on sore areas of the mouth is comforting.

Keep your mouth and gums clean to prevent infections. Check with your dentist often.

Things to Avoid

Avoid very hot foods.

Avoid other foods and drinks that would irritate your mouth, such as

- ❖ alcoholic beverages
- ❖ tart or acidic fruits or juices
- ❖ fresh pineapple
- ❖ raw walnuts
- ❖ dry or hard foods, such as crackers or toast
- ❖ course or fibrous foods such as bran, nuts, granola, and raw vegetables
- ❖ spicy foods
- ❖ very salty foods

"I have a major problem with constipation."

Problems with constipation are common. Constipation may be a result of taking some medications, especially pain medications, or may result from inadequate fluid or fiber intake or a lack of exercise. To prevent constipation, drink lots of fluids and include more fiber in your diet. Commercial soluble fiber products, laxatives, stool softeners, and other medications are available. These include

❖ Bulk forming products—Citrucel, Metamucil, FiberCon
❖ Stimulants—Correctol, Ex-Lax, Dulcolax, Senokot
❖ Stool softeners—Colace, Dialose, Surfak
❖ Lubricants—mineral oil
❖ Osmotics (to produce a wetter, softer stool)—Milk of magnesia, Lactulose, epsom salts

General Suggestions

Treat any underlying disorders.

Develop good bowel habits.

Drink plenty of fluids (8 to 10 full glasses each day), but avoid caffeinated beverages.

Try drinking warm or hot beverages. This may help stimulate bowel movements. Prune juice is also helpful.

Take walks and exercise regularly.

Choose a well balanced diet.

Gradually increase intake of high-fiber foods.

If the above does not work, take a laxative.

Important: Check with your physician if constipation persists.

Suggestions for Increasing Fiber in Your Diet

Choose several servings of raw fruits and vegetables every day. Eat the skins when possible. Raw red bell pepper, rutabagas, jicama, radishes, cabbage, green beans, defrosted frozen peas, broccoli, cauliflower, carrots, and celery make good snack alternatives.

Choose whole grain bread rather than more finely ground white bread or highly refined cereal. Examples include whole wheat, dark rye, pumpernickel, and oatmeal bread, and muffins and quick breads made with bran, nuts, fruit, seeds, etc.

High-fiber cereals include bran, shredded wheat, whole grain, bulgar wheat, and granola.

Add one to two tablespoons of 100 percent bran or wheat germ to your favorite cereal and to other foods.

Select high-fiber snack foods such as trail mix, sesame bread sticks, date nut bread, oatmeal cookies, fig newtons, date or raisin bars, granola, prune bread, or whole grain chips.

Add dried fruits to your diet and commercial dried chips made from vegetables or fruits.

"I HAVE A PROBLEM WITH CONSTIPATION."

Prepare dips for vegetables and chips from pureed canned beans (pinto, black, kidney, or garbanzo beans).

Commercial psyllium products are available and, if used regularly, may help prevent constipation.

High-Fiber Foods
Goal: 25 to 35 grams per day

Beans
5 to 10 grams fiber (1/2-cup serving)

Black beans, cooked | Lima beans, cooked
Kidney beans, cooked | Pinto beans, cooked
Lentils, cooked | White beans, cooked

Vegetables
1 to 4 grams fiber (1/2-cup serving)

Asparagus | Peas
Beets | Peppers
Broccoli | Potatoes with skin
Brussels sprouts | Pumpkin
Carrots | Rhubarb
Cauliflower | Spinach
Celery | Squash
Corn | Sweet potatoes
Green beans | Turnips
Parsnips

Fruits
1.5 to 5 grams fiber (1/2-cup serving or 1 medium fruit)

Apple with skin | Oranges
Apricots | Peaches
Avocado | Pears
Bananas | Prunes
Berries | Raisins
Cranberries | Strawberries
Figs | Tangerines
Kiwi

Breads
more than 2 grams fiber per serving

Bread, whole grain | Popcorn
Crackers, graham | Rice, brown
Crackers, whole grain | Wild rice

Cereals

9 to 12 grams fiber (1/2-cup serving)

100% Bran	Bran Buds
All Bran	Fiber One

3 to 6 grams fiber (1/2-cup serving)

Bran Chex	Crunchy Bran
Bran Flakes	Fruit and Fiber
Bulgar Wheat	Oat Bran
Corn Bran	Raisin Bran
Cracked Wheat	Shredded Wheat

1 to 2 grams fiber (1/2–3/4-cup serving)

Cheerios	Puffed Wheat
Grapenuts	Wheaties
Oatmeal, cooked	

less than 1 gram fiber (3/4-cup serving)

Corn Flakes	Rice Krispies

24

"I have a problem with diarrhea."

Diarrhea is a temporary or long-lasting symptom of distress in the intestinal tract. Diarrhea has many causes, including chemotherapy, radiation therapy, drug reactions, infections, food sensitivity, or injury to the intestinal tract. When food and liquids pass quickly through the bowels, there is a loss of calories, water, and nutrients. This may cause dehydration and serious electrolyte imbalance. Potassium and sodium are electrolytes that may be lost. Contact your doctor if your diarrhea is severe, bloody, or lasts for more than a couple of days.

Fiber

A low-fiber diet may help decrease cramps and gas and may help you control diarrhea. If bowel movements become more frequent and softer than usual, it is time to start making some changes to your diet and decreasing the amount of fiber in your diet.

Grains
To reduce fiber in your diet

Choose breads, biscuits, soft buns, cereals, crackers, pasta, and other grain products made with white flour that do not contain additional high-fiber grain products.

Read food labels for accurate information on fiber content.

Choose low-fiber cereals such as corn flakes and Rice Krispies, Puffed Wheat, Puffed Rice, Cream of Rice, and Cream of Wheat.

Read food labels to find other low-fiber cereals with less than 1 gram per serving.

Avoid the following high-fiber grains and grain products

Bran	Peanut flour
Breads with added fiber	Rye flour
Brown rice	Soybean flour
Buckwheat	Whole oats
Mixed grain breads	Whole wheat flour
Oatmeal	Wild rice

Fruits

Eat fewer fruits and limit portion sizes.

Choose more juice instead. Dilute fruit juice with water or club soda.

Choose the lower-fiber fruits, and limit serving sizes as listed below.

less than 1.5 grams fiber per 1/2-cup serving of fresh or canned fruit, unless noted

Applesauce	Mandarin oranges
Apricots, 4 halves (fresh or dried)	Mango
Banana, 1/2 medium	Nectarine, 1/2 medium
Cantaloupe	Olives, 5 green or black
Cherries	Peach, peeled
Fruit cocktail, canned	Pineapple
Fruit juices, clear	Plums, friar or prune
Grapefruit sections	Tangerine, 1 medium
Grapes, green or red	Watermelon
Honeydew melon	

Avoid high-fiber fruits such as unpeeled apple, avocado, blueberries, oranges, and pears.

Avoid fruits with seeds, such as blackberries, strawberries, raspberries, and kiwi.

Avoid dried fruits, such as raisins, figs, dates, prunes, and cranberries.

Avoid pear nectar, prune juice, unfiltered apple juice, and juices with pulp.

Vegetables

Eat smaller portions of vegetables at one time. Vegetables may be served fresh or cooked.

Choose the lower-fiber vegetables, and limit serving size as listed below.

Less than 1.5 grams fiber per 1/2 cup fresh serving, unless noted. After measuring 1/2 cup of the fresh vegetable, the vegetable may be eaten raw or cooked.

Bean sprouts	Mushrooms

Cabbage	Onion
Cauliflower	Pepper
Celery	Potato, peeled
Chinese cabbage	Radishes
Cucumber, peeled	Squash, acorn, 1/4 cup
Eggplant	Sweet potato, 1/4 cup
Endive	Tomato
Escarole	Zucchini or summer squash,
Lettuce, iceberg or leaf	peeled

Avoid high-fiber vegetables such as broccoli, Brussels sprouts, carrots, corn, potatoes with skin, pumpkin, rhubarb, spinach, and turnip greens.

26   **Important Note:** It is important to limit serving sizes of the fruits and vegetables you eat to the serving sizes recommended above. Larger portions will provide larger amounts of fiber.

Legumes and Nuts

Avoid all beans and peas.

Avoid all nuts, peanut butter, nut butters, and spreads.

Milk Products

You may have developed a temporary intolerance to lactose, which can lead to diarrhea, gas, and cramps. Lactose is the natural sugar found in milk products.

To reduce the lactose in your diet

Eat or drink smaller amounts of milk products at one time. For example, drink 1/4 cup or 1/2 cup of milk instead of 1 cup with your meal.

Experiment with the amount of dairy products you can tolerate. You may need to limit your milk intake to 2 cups per day.

Often yogurt with live cultures is tolerated better than milk or cheese.

Try reduced-lactose products, such as low-lactose milk and cheese.

Try products such as Lactaid tablets or drops.

Fats

Foods that are high in fat may contribute to diarrhea and loose stools.

To reduce the fat in your diet

Choose lean meats, poultry, and vegetables that have been baked, broiled, steamed, or stir-fried without added fat.

Choose low-fat milk, yogurt, cheese, cottage cheese, and other dairy products as tolerated.

Avoid fried foods and foods served with creamy sauces.

Avoid casseroles and mixed pasta dishes with high-fat ingredients.

Caffeine

Caffeine may stimulate bowel movements.

To reduce the caffeine in your diet

Choose decaffeinated coffee and tea.

Drink decaffeinated soft drinks.

Spices

Most herbs and spices can be used to add flavor to foods to suit your tastes. Some very spicy foods could contribute to diarrhea. Watch out for foods made with curry, chili powder, or hot pepper sauces.

27

Fluids

It is important to replace fluids lost from diarrhea to prevent dehydration. Drink at least 8 to 10 cups of clear fluids a day. Drink even if you are not thirsty. Your thirst sensation is not a good indicator of how much you should drink. Try to drink small amounts, such as 1/2 cup, often throughout the day to meet your total fluid needs. Avoid caffeinated beverages.

Clear liquids to try include

Water, sparkling water, club soda, and seltzer

Fruit juices and fruit drinks. If you can see through it, it is a clear liquid. Juices such as prune juice and nectar are not clear liquids. Juice may be diluted with water or club soda.

Soft drinks that are caffeine-free

Weak decaffeinated tea and coffee

Clear soup and broth

Popsicles

Gelatin

Sweet Foods

Avoid large amounts of very sweet foods and liquids.

Avoid foods sweetened with sorbitol, such as sugar-free jelly, jam, candy, and gum.

Temperature of Fluids

Drinking fluids at room temperature may be helpful in reducing diarrhea or cramping. Hot or cold liquids may stimulate bowel movements. Avoid liquids that are very hot or very cold to see if this works for you.

Meal Size

Eat small amounts of food and drink small amounts of liquid throughout the day instead of three larger meals. Large amounts of food at one time may stimulate bowel movements.

Fiber Supplements

Water-soluble fiber supplements such as pectins (e.g. Sure-Jell) or commercial products (e.g. Metamucil) may help produce a firmer stool. These water-soluble fibers absorb bile salts, which are irritating to the intestinal tract. They may also thicken the stool and produce a firmer stool.

28

Salt Replacement

To replace lost salt, eat high-salt foods and liquids, such as broth, bouillon, pretzels, and cheese. Do not take salt pills, which can lead to dangerously high levels of sodium.

Potassium Replacement

To replace lost potassium, choose high-potassium foods and liquids, such as bananas, baked or boiled potatoes, orange juice, pineapple juice, tomato juice, and meat.

Persistent Diarrhea

If diarrhea persists, try limiting your intake to only the following foods: bananas, white rice, Cream of Rice, mashed potatoes, peeled apples, yogurt with live cultures, decaffeinated tea, white toast, plain bagels, noodles, eggs, and lean meat or poultry without added fats. Try this just for a few days, then contact your physician if bowel movements continue to be very loose, watery, and frequent.

Electrolyte Replacement Solutions

If diarrhea is severe, use special electrolyte replacement fluids that are commercially available or make your own electrolyte replacement solution.

Homemade Electrolyte Replacement Solution (for adults)

1 teaspoon salt
1 teaspoon baking soda
1 tablespoon corn syrup

6-ounce can frozen orange juice concentrate
6 cups water

Mix all ingredients together. Refrigerate. Shake or stir well before serving.

By choosing the foods and beverages suggested in this section, you will be better able to manage the symptoms of diarrhea and yet eat a balanced diet. It is important to eat enough to provide your body with sufficient nutrients for maintaining weight and healing and repairing body tissues. Once diarrhea has settled down, you should slowly add foods that had been omitted back into your diet.

Check with your physician immediately if you have symptoms of dehydration.

"I'm gaining too much weight."

Weight gain may occur during treatment of some forms of cancer. It is especially common among women after the diagnosis of breast cancer. Although it is extremely important to maintain good nutritional health and avoid weight loss with cancer, it is also important to prevent significant weight gain. Weight gain may be caused by the cancer, cancer treatments, or psychological stresses. Some women with breast cancer seem to experience food cravings similar to those of pregnant women. Other women who experience nausea find that eating more often decreases the nausea symptoms but the secondary effect is weight gain. Weight gain can be demoralizing. Coping with the diagnosis of cancer and making all of the critical decisions for treatment plans cause enough psychological stress without adding the problems related to gaining unwanted weight.

Recent studies of women with breast cancer suggest that weight gain during therapy may increase the risk of cancer recurrence and decrease survival rates. Various theories have been proposed to explain these negative effects associated with weight gain. One theory suggests that there are increased levels of free, circulating estrogens when body weight increases. Free estrogens have a role in the development of some breast cancers. Another theory suggests that the body's immune system does not function up to par when there is excess body weight. (Demark-Wahnefried, W., Rimer, B. and Winer, E. "Weight gain in women diagnosed with breast cancer," J. American Dietetic Assoc. 97:519–526, May 1997)

Some forms of chemotherapy, such as high dose steroids used to treat lymphomas, can cause a form of weight gain that is due to water retention, not from eating excess calories. Notify your doctor if you have rapid and uncomfortable weight gain as this may be water retention and may respond to diuretics, not decreased food intake.

Weight management plays an important role in cancer survival. To remember helpful hints for healthy eating and weight control, use the acronym

29

V I C T O R Y

Vegetables and fruits are number one!

Ignore "secret" weight loss formulas and fad diets.

Calories do count.

Take the time to enjoy your food.

Order carefully when eating out.

Read labels and nutritional analyses.

You make the choices.

Vegetables and fruits are number one!

Eating vegetables and fruits should be a priority of you are struggling with weight gain. They provide nutrients and phytochemicals to help fight cancer and help with weight control, too.

Try to eat five to nine servings of fruits and vegetables every day. Choose a variety of fruits and vegetables. Each one has its own unique makeup. By eating a variety, they will provide you with many vitamins, minerals, and plant chemicals (phytochemicals) that will enhance your nutritional health and improve your immune system.

Research is underway to identify which plant foods and which components of plant foods help prevent and fight cancer. There are no definitive answers at this time. But preliminary results suggest that some of the most important fruits and vegetables to include in your diet are: broccoli, Brussels sprouts, cauliflower, cabbage, spinach, chard, greens, carrots, squash, peppers, onions, garlic, tomatoes, oranges, grapefruit, kiwi, mangos, cantaloupe, and berries.

Eat them the way you like them. It really isn't necessary to eat them raw. Raw fruits and vegetables are great, but most nutrients are not destroyed by cooking. In fact, some nutrients are more available for absorption after foods are cooked.

Eat fruits and vegetables at every meal and find new ways of preparing them. They can be part of every course from appetizer to dessert. They make refreshing, healthy snacks, too.

Ignore "secret" weight loss formulas and fad diets.

There is no magic diet or formula or pill that will guarantee weight control or weight loss.

Most diets that are promoted in the current best selling books provide new twists on old diets that did not work in the past. If there really was a secret diet, we would all soon learn about it and there would be no need for yet another diet book.

Many fad diets are deficient in some essential nutrients. This is true of any diet that limits your selection of foods or dictates specific food combinations. It is extremely important while you are fighting cancer not to stress your body with a diet that is low in essential nutrients or contains an unnatural balance of nutrients.

Diets do not work because they make you feel deprived and crabby. Diets are usually something you go on temporarily, and you tend to live for the day when you can go off your diet. Do not spend your life going off and on diets. Form good, sensible eating habits and this will be the ideal diet for life.

Calories do count.

Weight is a matter of the balance between calories in and calories out.

Become aware of the caloric value of the foods you eat often. If you are tired and lack energy, you may be using fewer calories. You may have gained weight even though you are not eating any more than usual.

Use lower-fat alternatives in place of high-fat foods.

Try reduced-fat modified recipes and use as little fat in cooking as possible.

Limit the fat in your diet, but be aware that counting only fat grams is not the total answer to weight control. Low-fat foods can fool you. Some low-fat foods are actually high in calories.

Increase the fiber in your diet to help you feel full without adding lots of calories. Foods rich in fiber include whole fruits and vegetables (instead of juice), whole grains, high-fiber cereals, and dried beans, split peas, lentils, and other legumes.

Surround yourself with low-calorie snack foods at home or work. Avoid having high-calorie snack foods around. Making food harder to get forces you to make a deliberate decision to eat.

Don't forget about the calories in the beverages you choose. Calories in fruit juice add up quickly. Flavored bottled water and ice tea can be high in calories. Check labels.

Don't use high-calorie foods to reward yourself. One high-calorie treat can negate all your good choices from the rest of the day.

Budget your calories and use them wisely. If a food isn't very tasty and not worth the calories, don't eat it.

Take the time to enjoy your food.

One of life's greatest pleasures is eating. Choose foods you really like.

Slow down when you eat. Listen to soothing music to help you slow down.

Stop in the middle of your meal to check your hunger and appetite. Wait a few minutes before deciding if you need more food.

Be aware of what you are eating. Activities such as reading or watching television may distract you while eating and you may end up eating more than you had planned to eat.

Savor your food. If the food is especially good but high in calories, limit the amount you eat and enjoy every bite.

32

Order carefully when eating out.

Restaurant meals are notorious for being high in calories and high in fat but there are usually some good choices on the menu. When deciding where to go out to eat, make it a point to choose restaurants that provide a variety of healthy choices.

Make your menu choices carefully. Ask questions about how foods are prepared.

Salads are not always low-calorie choices. Although you can create a healthy low-calorie salad from a salad bar, some selections are high in calories or fat. Watch out for bacon bits, cheese, seeds, fried croutons, pasta with mayonnaise dressing, potato salads, and regular dressings.

Ask for low-fat or low-calorie dressings and sauce on the side. *You* be in charge of how much you will use.

Watch out for the extras suggested by your server.

Order small or half-size portions or share a meal with a friend.

Don't give in to pressure from fellow diners to eat foods you really would like to avoid.

Watch out for alcoholic beverages. Alcoholic drinks add calories and reduce inhibitions. You may end up eating more than you intended.

Read labels and nutritional analyses.

Food labels give a wealth of information. Check for calories, fat, and other nutrients that are of interest to you. Do not assume that a label stating "low fat" or "healthy" mean low calories.

Pay special attention to serving size. What may seem like a single serving to you may actually be labeled for two or more servings on the package. Adjust your calorie count accordingly.

Use the label to budget your calories. Evaluate the food by asking, "Is this particular food worth the calories? Is it a good source of nutrients?"

In this cookbook and other cookbooks, check nutrient analysis for calories and fat in the recipes before making your selections.

You make the choices.

You are in charge of your nutritional health. Focus on behavior changes rather than diet changes.

Concentrate on improving your overall health by improving your eating habits with small changes.

Listen to your body cues and eat when you are hungry, and most importantly, stop when you are full.

It is difficult to make good choices if you get ravenously hungry. The hungrier you are, the harder it is to resist temptations at a cocktail party or a buffet table or even standing in front of your own refrigerator.

Consider your new eating habit changes to be part of a healthy new lifestyle. Do not go on a restrictive diet or make changes that are very unpleasant or uncomfortable for you. Be sensible in your choices and you will continue them for a lifetime.

Identify foods that you really enjoy and budget them into your eating plan.

Include daily exercise. Exercise is crucial to weight maintenance. Any amount is better than none and you don't have to exercise for long periods of time. Exercising several times a day for 10 minutes each time is beneficial, too.

Take walks in the fresh air. It will make you feel better. Walking is the easiest form of exercise. It requires no special equipment and you can walk anywhere. Find a walking partner or walk the dog.

Adopt a sensible and enjoyable eating and exercise plan to enhance your life.

Cancer-Fighting Fruits and Vegetables

This discussion is a summary of current scientific information relating vegetables and fruit to cancer prevention and treatment as reported by Dr. Kristi Steinmetz and Dr. John Potter in the Journal of the American Dietetic Association, *October 1996.*

Throughout history, people have lived well when their diets were rich in fruits and vegetables. There has always been an intuitive belief that these foods are special and are good for the body. Now science has proven without a doubt that there is a strong relationship between the intake of fruits and vegetables and health.

For one thing, fruits and vegetables are helpful in fighting cancer once it has developed. More than 20 animal studies have been conducted in which cancer has been experimentally induced by means of chemical or irradiation effects in mice, rats, or hamsters. These animals were then fed specified amounts of certain vegetables and fruits—mainly cruciferous vegetables, soy products, citrus oils, or allium vegetables. In the majority of these studies, it was found that the animals fed fruits and vegetables experienced fewer tumors, smaller tumors, fewer metastases, less DNA damage, or higher levels of enzymes involved in the detoxification of carcinogens.

It is important to note that results of animal studies do not always apply to humans, but these studies give us hope that there is something we can do to fight cancer even after it has developed. Eating fruits and vegetables also has been shown to *protect* us from some forms of heart disease and cancer.

The evidence for decreasing cancer risk by eating fruits and vegetables is especially strong for stomach cancer. The most important foods associated with the reduction of stomach cancer are citrus fruits and raw green vegetables. For colon cancer, the best protectors are raw vegetables and green vegetables. All fruits and vegetables that contain dietary fiber are also helpful in preventing colon cancer because fiber binds potential carcinogens and bile acids and helps with their excretion from the colon. Bile acids can be an irritant to the colon. Dietary fiber is also fermented by bacteria in the colon, which leads to the production of short-chained fatty acids. This acid environment protects against some cancer-causing substances.

For cancers of the esophagus, oral cavity, and pharynx, green vegetables and citrus fruits consistently appear to be protective. Tomatoes appear to be protective against esophageal cancer and prostate cancer and carrots against cancers of the oral cavity and pharynx. For rectal cancer, the evidence of a protective effect of cruciferous vegetables is most prominent. For breast cancer, the data show a benefit from the consumption of fruits, green vegetables, and carrots. Lung cancer protection has been associated with all fruits and vegetables.

For all the benefits of fruits and vegetables, Americans eat an average of only three and one-half servings of fruits and vegetables per day. Only about 20 percent of Americans eat the recommended five or more servings per day. We could fight cancer by changing our eating habits and eating more fruits and vegetables.

Fruits and Vegetables Protect Against Cancer by

acting as antioxidants

promoting normal cell growth

increasing activity of enzymes that detoxify carcinogens

blocking formation of nitrosamines

altering the bacteria and pH in the colon

preserving the integrity of cells

maintaining and repairing DNA

increasing the death rate of cancer cells

decreasing the multiplication of cancer cells

altering estrogen metabolism

The types of vegetables or fruits that most often appear to be protective against cancer are the following:

Allium vegetables

Onions, garlic, scallions, shallots, leeks, and chives are rich in organic sulfur compounds that have been shown to increase the activity of enzymes involved in the detoxification of cancer-causing substances. These compounds may also inhibit certain bacteria that help convert nitrates to nitrites in the stomach. Nitrites can combine with amines to form nitrosamines, which may be carcinogenic, particularly in the stomach.

Cruciferous vegetables

Broccoli, cauliflower, Brussels sprouts, and cabbage are unique in their high content of two organic compounds containing sulfur (dithiolthiones and isothiocyanates) which have been shown to increase the activity of enzymes involved in detoxifying some carcinogens and other foreign compounds. Cruciferous vegetables also contain indol-3-carbinol, which affects estrogen metabolism and may protect against estrogen-related cancers, such as breast and endometrial cancers.

Green vegetables

Lettuce, kale, spinach, mustard greens, and other green leafy vegetables contain lutein, carotenoid, and xanthophyll, which act as antioxidants. Antioxidants may protect against cancer by their ability to block damage from free radicals within a cell. Green leafy vegetables are also a rich source of folic acid, which is a vitamin that may protect cells from chromosomal damage.

Orange and yellow fruits and vegetables

Cantaloupe, papaya, mango, carrots, sweet potatoes, winter squash, and pumpkins are relatively rich sources of beta carotene. Beta carotene is an antioxidant and it can also be metabolized to vitamin A, which helps to maintain healthy cells.

Red fruits and vegetables

Tomatoes, red bell peppers, raspberries are particularly rich in a red pigment that is a lycopene. Lycopenes act as antioxidants.

Citrus fruits

Oranges, grapefruit, tangerines, lemons, and limes are rich in vitamin C, which acts as an antioxidant to protect cell membranes and DNA from oxidative damage. Vitamin C may further help prevent cancer by preventing the formation of nitrosamines. Citrus fruits also contain coumarins and limonene, which have been shown to increase the activity of other detoxifying enzymes.

Soybeans

Soybeans are unique in their content of isoflavones, which are weak estrogen-like compounds that are found in plants. These compounds compete with more potent estrogens for binding to estrogen receptors in breast tissue. By this mechanism, isoflavones may inhibit estrogen-promoted breast cancer. In fact, certain plant estrogens are similar to tamoxifen, a drug that is used to treat some breast cancer and is currently being tested for cancer prevention in high-risk women. One particular isoflavone, genistein, has been shown to inhibit the activity of an enzyme involved in cancer cell growth. Soybeans also contain protease inhibitors, saponins, phytosterols, and other compounds that have been shown to stop cancer in animal studies. The saponins may exert a preventive effect against colon cancer by binding bile acids and cholesterol in the colon.

Herbal Remedies

Plants have been used for thousands of years to alleviate a variety of symptoms and diseases. A renewed interest in preventive medicine has driven many people back to these ancient herbal products in search of more "natural" remedies. More and more people are using botanicals as complements to, or substitutes for, conventional drug therapy.

Information coming out of current research on the benefits of various phytochemicals in foods supports the possibility that certain chemical compounds in herbs could be helpful in the prevention and treatment of cancer. Taxol is an example of a drug we use in cancer treatment that comes from a plant source.

Technically, herbs are just the leaves of plants, but the bark, stems, roots, flowers, and extracts of certain plants are commonly referred to as herbs, also. Herbs are available fresh or dried. Manufacturers produce them as pills, liquid extracts, tinctures, ointments, and teas.

Can Herbs Prevent or Treat Cancer Effectively?

If there was an herb that prevented or cured cancer, we would all use it and never deal with this terrible disease again. It is possible that an herb can work with your body and make your treatments more effective. It is also possible that an herb can work against you and cause serious complications. The challenge is to determine what has promise and what is potentially harmful.

The tables starting on pages 39 and 43 are beginning guidelines to the use of herbs, but it will always be hard for both consumers and health professionals to weed out the good herbs from the bad. The companies that sell herbs aren't always much help because the Food and Drug Administration (FDA) does not require them to print possible side effects on the labels.

Most people believe that any product that appears in pill form has been reviewed for safety by the FDA. This is not true for herbal supplements. Botanicals do not have to be proved safe before they are put on store shelves. It's only after a problem occurs that a product is withdrawn. FDA officials cannot remove an herb from the market unless they can prove beyond a doubt that the product is unsafe. It is the responsibility of the manufacturer to provide "reasonable assurance" that no ingredient presents a significant or unreasonable risk of illness or injury.

It is important to know that the manufacturer does not have to prove a product is not harmful before selling it. Of the roughly 600 botanicals sold in the United States, fewer than a dozen have been tested in noteworthy clinical trials, which determine whether an herb is safe and works better than a placebo.

Herbs are regulated much less strictly than drugs, so there are no stringent standards for controlling their quality, content, concentration, or dose recommendations. There are no guarantees that label information on pills or tonics is reliable; however, the industry is in the process of adopting rules to prevent giving misleading information to consumers.

It is difficult to find consistent products on the market. There can be great variations in what the label states and what is actually in the product. It is also common for plants to be improperly identified by the manufacturer. Some herbal preparations have been found to be contaminated with microorganisms, fungi, aflotoxins, metal contaminants, and even other medications.

Some reliable books and resources provide good information about herbs (see the listing at the end of this section), but be cautious of literature promoting the sale of a product. It is illegal for claims on supplements to state that the herb will cure or prevent a disease, but the claim can detail how the herb affects the body's structure or function. For instance, a claim cannot state that an herb cures cancer, but it can state that it enhances the immune system to fight cancer. The name of the product can also be designed to imply a health benefit, such as "Sleep Easy."

Testimonials of cancer cures by real people are impelling, but a testimonial does not necessarily give the whole picture. People with cancer have varying survival times, and any remedy that is used by a large number of people can be expected to be used by someone who will be a long-term survivor. That person may credit the herb, but it is not necessarily the herb that prolonged life.

38

What About Herbal Teas?

Herbal teas may be special taste treats, but they are not actually real tea. True tea comes from the leaves of a green, bushy shrub known as the tea plant. Green, black, and oolong tea all come from this plant. The difference between them has to do with how they are processed.

Herbal tea can be made from any plant and any part of the plant. Each tea has its own unique flavor and possible medicinal value. Some appear to relieve symptoms like an upset stomach, sore throat, stuffy nose, or insomnia. Herbal teas may indeed safely deliver what they promise. Sometimes, however, manufacturers overstep their bounds, implying curative powers that are unproven or simply untrue. Also, some herbs, such as echinacea and ginkgo, may be effective in concentrated pill forms but they are worthless as teas. The ingredients that are thought to be the active ingredients are not water-soluble, so they do not leach into the water from the tea bag. In some cases, the concentration needed for a beneficial effect is much higher than you could get from a tea solution.

While many herbal teas are too weak to be effective, others contain potent compounds that can be harmful. Hawthorne can lower blood pressure, senna leaf can cause diarrhea, and ma huang contains ephedra, which can cause insomnia, nervousness, dangerously high blood pressure, and even death. Teas made from comfrey, coltsfoot, chaparral, and germander are suspected of causing liver cancer.

Most commercially prepared, nationally-available herbal teas are probably safe in reasonable amounts, but, because they are not regulated by the FDA, there is no guarantee that the herb you think you are buying is actually in the product or present in the amount stated on the label. It would be prudent not to consume the same kind of herbal tea daily for more than two or three days at a time. Read package warnings about who should avoid the product.

(Welland, D., "Herbal teas brew up proven benefits, potential risks,"
Environmental Nutrition, October 1996)

Knowing the Best and Safe Dose of an Herb

The question of how much is too much depends on the herb and your treatment regimen. Each herb has its own safe dose. Some herbs, such as belladonna, are deadly even in low doses. Other herbs, such as St. John's-wort, can be taken safely only in small amounts, and some, such as chamomile, are safe in larger amounts. If a substance is toxic, the liver has a better chance of detoxifying it if you take it in small amounts. Toxicities, however, do build up over months or years. Toxins called pyrolizidine alkaloids in comfrey, coltsfoot, and borage will damage the liver over time.

It is possible that certain herbal supplements may really work to help you fight cancer. There may be active pharmacological agents in the herbs that could be of benefit to you.

Still, there are risks. The greatest potential dangers in the use of traditionally nontoxic herbs are: (1) the risk of contamination, misidentification, or substitution with a harmful plant, (2) the lack of quality control of the products, and (3) the potential adverse effects when combined with chemotherapy.

The use of herbs can give you a sense of control when faced with a cancer diagnosis. This can be very beneficial to you in the fight against cancer. It is crucial, however, to work with your physician if you are taking herbs so you are not setting the stage for adverse interactions with your other treatments.

There is no one best piece of advice for everyone. Although botanical remedies hold great promise, the use of herbs is a personal decision. Since there is no governmental approval and regulation of herbs for medicinal use, it is best to use herbs with caution.

Herbs with Documented Harmful Effects

This is not designed to be a complete list. Do not assume an herb is safe if it is not included here. The majority of herbs and mixtures of herbs have not been safety tested.

Common Name	Other Names	Reason for Caution
Aconite	Monkshood Bushi	Numerous poisonings in China

Common Name	Other Names	Reason for Caution
Arnica	Wolfsbane Mountain tobacco	Fatal poisonings reported with internal use: cardiac toxicity. External use acceptable but rashes possible. (1,2)
Belladonna	Deadly nightshade	Contains three toxic alkaloids, one of which is atropine. (1,2)
Blue cohosh	Squaw root	Potential for toxic effects of heart muscle and intestinal spasms. (1)
Borage		May contain liver toxins and carcinogens. (1)
Broom	Broom tops Irish broom	Contains toxic alkaloids and tyramine. Danger of mold contamination in flowers. May slow heart rhythm. (1,2)
Calamus	Sweet root Sweet flag	Certain types containing isoasarone are carcinogenic. (1,2)
Chaparral	Creosote bush	Responsible for at least 6 cases of hepatitis, with 1 person requiring a liver transplant. (3,4)
Coltsfoot		Contains a liver toxin (pyrrolizidine alkaloid called senkirkine), which is also a carcinogen. (1)
Comfrey		Contains liver toxins (pyrrolizidine alkaloids) linked to liver disease and possible death. Organ problems and cancer seen in animal studies. (3,5)
Convallaria	Lily of the valley	Contains toxic cardiac glycosides. (1,2)
Ephedra	Ephedrine Epitonin Ma huang	Stimulant that can induce heart palpitations, high blood pressure, stroke, psychosis, etc. (6) Several deaths and hundreds of adverse reports have been reported to FDA.

40

Common Name	Other Names	Reason for Caution
Germander	Germanium	Marketed as a folk medicine for weight loss. (7) Linked to cases of liver inflammation, kidney damage, and death. (5)
Jimsonweed		Contains potentially toxic alkaloids, such as atropine. (2)
Jin bu huan		Reported cases of hepatitis. (8) Three children developed respiratory depression with slow pulse rate. (9)
Laetrile	Vitamin B17	Tested and found ineffective in cancer therapy; can result in cyanide poisoning if ingested. (Vitamin B17 is not a recognized vitamin.)
Licorice		If used in excess, potential for high blood pressure, low potassium, and cardiac arrest. (1)
Liferoot	Golden senecio Ragwort	Can induce liver disease and malignancies. (1)
Lobelia	Indian tobacco Wild tobacco	Reports of respiratory depression, rapid heartbeat, low blood pressure, coma, convulsions, and death. (1,5)
Kombucha	Kombucha tea	Fermentation of various yeast and bacteria in a mixture of black tea and sugar. Prone to contamination.
Mandrake		Poisonous narcotic similar to belladonna. A strong hallucinogen. (2)

Common Name	Other Names	Reason for Caution
Mistletoe	Iscador	Although research is being done in other countries for its potential in cancer chemotherapy, it is still considered highly toxic and not considered safe for normal consumption. (1) The mistletoe berry is poisonous.
Pau d'Arco		Produces severe side effects at effective levels and may interfere with blood clotting. (10)
Pennyroyal Oil		Especially toxic. Liver damage, convulsions, abortions, coma, and death reported. (1)
Periwinkle		Toxic to liver and other body cells. Contains the chemotherapy agents vincristine and vinblastine, which need physician dosing and monitoring. (2)
Poke root		Extremely toxic. Deaths, gastroenteritis, low blood pressure, and reduced respiration reported. (1)
Sassafras		Contains a carcinogen, safrole, banned by FDA for food use, but sold in health food stores as a supplement. (1)
Skullcap		Liver damage reports and potential for adulteration. (1)
Wormwood	Madder Mugwort Mingwort	Extreme mind-altering effects. Convulsions, unconsciousness. (1,2)
Yohimbe		Monoamine oxidase inhibitor (MAO), which can increase blood pressure if certain foods are not avoided. Reports of psychoses, paralysis, fatigue, kidney failure, death. (1,5)

42

Adapted from Spaulding-Albright, N. "A Review of Some Herbal and Related Products Commonly Used in Cancer Patients," Copyright Oncology Nutrition Dietetic Practice Group of The American Dietetic Association. Reprinted with permission from *ON-LINE,* Volume 5, Number 2, 1997.

References

1. Tyler, V.E. *The Honest Herbal.* Binghamton, NY: Pharmaceutical Products Press Publishers; 1993.

2. "Unsafe herbs." *FDA Consumer.* October 1983.

3. "Herbal roulette." *Consumer Reports.* November 1995.

4. Gordon, D.W., Rosenthal, G., Hart, J., Sirota, R., Baker, A.L. "Chaparral ingestion: the broadening spectrum of liver injury caused by herbal medications." *JAMA.* 1995; 273:489–490.

5. Kessler, D. "Unsubstantiated Claims and Documented Health Hazards in the Dietary Supplement Marketplace." *FDA presentation at the Subcommittee on Health and the Environment,* July 29, 1993, pp. 100–105.

6. *FDA Statement on Street Drugs Containing Botanical Ephedrine,* April 10, 1996.

7. Larrey, D., Vial, T., Panwek, A., Castor, A., Biour, M., David, M., Michel, H. "Hepatitis after germander administration: another instance of herbal medicine hepatotoxicity." *Ann Intern Med* 1992; 117:129–132.

8. Woolf, G.M., Petrovic, L.M., Rojter, S.E., Wainwright, S., Villamil, F.G., Katkov, W.N., Michieletti, P., Wanless, I.P., Stermitx, F.R., Beck, J.J., Vierling, J.M. "Acute hepatitis associated with the Chinese herbal product jin bu huan." *Ann Intern Med* 1994; 121:729–735.

9. Horowitz, R.S., Dart, R.C., Gormez, H., Moore, L.L., Fulton, B. "Jin bu huan toxicity in children—Colorado, 1993." *Morbid Mortal Weekly Rep.* 1993; 43:633–635.

10. *American Cancer Society.* "Questionable methods of cancer management." *Nutritional Therapies.* 1993.

Herbs with Promising Benefits and Reasonably Strong Evidence of Safety

It is important to note that these herbs may not be helpful for cancer prevention or treatment. Many of the claims made about the herbs have not been studied or tested.

Common Name	Other Names	Claims
Astragalus	Huang-chi	May stimulate immune system. May stimulate production of interferon. Overdosing may cause suppression of the immune system.

43

Common Name	Other Names	Claims
Cat's Claw		May have low level antioxidant activity. High in tannins, which may interfere with absorption of nutrients. Adulteration is common, which can lead to harmful effects.
Chamomile		Claims to soothe an upset stomach. Possible adverse reaction if allergic to ragweed.
Echinacea	Coneflower	May stimulate the immune system. May cause reactions if allergic to sunflower family.
Feverfew		Claims to give headache relief. Main side effect is irritation and possible inflammation of the lining of the mouth.
Essiac and Phytaid		Trade names for combination of herbs. Products under study.
Garlic		Claims to reduce blood cholesterol and prevent cancer.
Ginger		May reduce chemotherapy-induced nausea. Can inhibit blood clotting if taken in large amounts.
Ginkgo		Claims to improve memory and other mental functions.
Ginseng		Claims to increase vitality. Expensive.
Peppermint		Claims to help quell nausea.
Silymarin	Milk thistle Marian Our Lady's thistle	Extracted from artichoke. May stimulate protein synthesis. May have antioxidant properties. Claims to be an antitumor agent.
Shiitake Mushrooms		May contain lentinan, an antitumor carbohydrate.
St. John's-Wort		Claims to be an antidepressant.

Common Name	Other Names	Claims
Valerian		Claims to have calming effects on emotions.

Adapted from Spaulding-Albright, N. "A Review of Some Herbal and Related Products Commonly Used in Cancer Patients," Copyright Oncology Nutrition Dietetic Practice Group of The American Dietetic Association. Reprinted with permission from *ON-LINE*, Volume 5, Number 2.

Helpful Resources

American Botanical Council, Austin, TX
512/331-8868
http://www.herbalgram.org/abcmission.html

Environmental Nutrition Newsletter, Palm Coast, FL
800/829-5384

Food and Drug Administration, Rockville, MD
800/332-0178
http://www.fda.gov/fdahomepage.html

Herb Research Foundation, Boulder, CO
303/449-2265
http://www.sunsite.unc.edu/herbs/

Herbs of Choice—The Therapeutic Use of Phytomedicinals, by Varro Tyler, Pharmaceutical Products Press, 1994

The Honest Herbal, 3rd Edition, by Varro Tyler, Pharmaceutical Products Press, 1993

National Council Against Health Fraud, Loma Linda, CA
909/824-4690

Office of Alternative Medicine, NIH, Bethesda, MD
800/531-1794

Neutropenic Precautions Diet

Neutropenia is a low neutrophil count. Neutrophils are one of five types of white blood cells. Of the five types of white blood cells, neutrophils are the most important for fighting infections. A normal white blood cell count is 3,500 to 10,000. A normal neutrophil count is 1,600 to 7,000. If the neutrophil count is less than 1,000 there is an increased risk for infection.

Neutropenia can be caused by chemotherapy, radiation therapy, or your disease. When the neutrophil count is depressed, it is important to decrease your risk of infection. Some adjustments are needed in your diet to prevent food-borne illness from harmful bacteria and fungi.

It is important to note that this diet does not provide enough folic acid. With long-term use of this diet, a multivitamin/mineral supplement should be used.

Allowed	Not Allowed
Meat, Poultry, Fish, Dry Beans, Eggs, Nuts	
All well cooked meat, poultry, fish	Rare to medium cooked meat, poultry, fish
Cooked beans	Raw beans
Well cooked eggs	Runny or undercooked eggs
Roasted nuts	Raw nuts
Milk & Dairy	
All pasteurized milk and dairy products	Yogurt with live cultures
Yogurt without live cultures	Yogurt with dried fruit
Bread, Cereal, Rice, Pasta	
All cooked or baked grain products	Cereal with raisins or dried fruit
Cooked pasta dishes	
Vegetables	
All cooked vegetables	All raw vegetables
Fruits	
All cooked or canned fruit and juice.	Fresh fruits other than those noted
Oranges, grapefruit, bananas, and melons can be eaten if they are washed and then peeled carefully.	Dried fruit unless used as an ingredient in baked products
	Fresh squeezed juice
Spices	
Spices may be used as an ingredient only in well-cooked products.	Pepper and other dry spices or herbs that are sprinkled on food after it is cooked.

46

Protect Your Food, Protect Yourself

Safe handling, cooking, and serving of food is necessary to prevent bacteria and other microorganisms from multiplying and causing food poisoning. People with weakened immune systems need to be especially careful to take steps to minimize the risk of contracting a food-borne illness. The following food-handling tips will help lower the risk of potential food contamination for all.

Safe food handling begins with frequent and careful hand washing.

Wash hands by lathering with soap and warm water after using the restroom, blowing your nose, handling garbage, changing baby diapers, touching or cleaning up after any kind of pet, before handling food, and between handling raw and cooked foods. Also, clean nails with a nailbrush before handling food and after handling raw poultry, meat, or fish. Bacteria and debris can become lodged under the nails and be a source for food contamination. If you have diarrhea, wash hands very carefully with antibacterial soap and wear disposable plastic gloves if you prepare food. Be careful that small children in the family wash their hands and be cautious about accepting food from children who may not have washed their hands.

If you are on chemotherapy or are having radiation treatments to the head and neck, hair loss can be a problem. Wear a scarf, turban, or hair net when preparing meals to avoid finding hair in your food. You will not lose your appetite by an unpleasant discovery in your soup or salad!

At the Grocery Store

Check expiration dates on foods, and do not buy or use if the food is out of date.

Place raw meat and poultry packages in plastic bags to prevent leakage on other groceries.

If you have a choice, purchase ground meat at a grocery store where the meat is ground on site. The process of grinding the meat increases the surface area of the meat and accelerates the potential for bacterial contamination from numerous sources. Ground meat and poultry that is commercially packaged before reaching the grocery store may have a higher bacterial content than meat ground at the grocery store. Meat ground at the grocery store is more likely to be exposed to a cleaner environment than at the packing plant and it is usually fresher.

If food will be held in a warm car for longer than 30 minutes, keep perishable foods in a cooler to keep them cold.

Do not buy or use canned goods that are swollen, dented, or otherwise damaged.

Do not buy frozen foods that have thawed.

Storing Food

Keep perishable foods in a refrigerator that is 35° to 40°F or in a freezer at 0°F or below.

Place uncooked meat, fish, and poultry in separate plastic bags and place in the refrigerator so juices cannot drip onto or come in contact with other foods.

Thaw meat in the refrigerator, not on the counter.

Food stored in the freezer needs to be wrapped in freezer bags or freezer paper.

Defrosted foods should be cooked soon after the defrosting is complete. Food may be refrozen only if it still has ice crystals.

Refrigerate leftovers immediately in covered containers. For more rapid cooling, use small, shallow containers. Foods placed in the refrigerator in large containers may stay warm in the center of the pan for a dangerously long time.

Arrange food in the refrigerator so the cool air can circulate around the food containers.

Remove stuffing from poultry or meats and refrigerate in separate containers.

Throw out refrigerated leftovers after three to four days.

Do not eat moldy food. You can save hard cheese and firm fruits and vegetables by cutting the mold out along with a large area around the mold. All other moldy food should be discarded.

Do not taste or eat food with an unusual odor or if it looks strange.

Preparing Food

Keep everything that touches food clean—hands, utensils, bowls, countertops, dishcloths, etc.

Use separate plates, cutting boards, knives, and utensils for raw and cooked meat, poultry, and fish. It's best to use one cutting board for meat and a separate one for fruits and vegetables.

Keep juices from raw meat, poultry, and fish from coming into contact with all other foods.

Cook meat, poultry, and fish thoroughly. Red meat is well done at 160°F or when brown or gray inside. Poultry should be cooked to 180°F or until it is no longer pink and juices run clear. Fish should be cooked until it changes color and flakes with a fork.

Cook hamburgers and any ground meats until brown throughout and juices run clear. If meat remains pink, cook it again before eating. Ground meats should reach an internal temperature of 160°F.

Cook stuffing separately from poultry. The cavity of a turkey or chicken may not get hot enough to thoroughly cook the ingredients in the stuffing. The raw juices from the poultry that are released during the cooking process into the stuffing may not be thoroughly cooked.

If you are using pork sausage or other ground raw meats in a stuffing or dressing, be sure they are thoroughly cooked before mixing with the other ingredients. This has two purposes. The time and temperature needed to cook the raw meat in the dressing or stuffing may not be long enough to kill harmful bacteria, especially if the stuffing is in a rolled meat. The other reason is to remove the excess fat from the product so it does not make the stuffing too greasy.

Do not eat hot dogs without thoroughly heating. Hot dogs can harbor *Listeria monocytogenes*, a bacteria that can make immunocompromised persons sick. The bacteria is destroyed by cooking.

Never eat undercooked or raw eggs or foods that may contain undercooked or raw eggs, such as homemade mayonnaise, some Caesar salad dressings (commercially prepared products are safe), cookie dough, and desserts that contain raw eggs, such as mousse made from scratch.

Never taste any mixture that has raw meat, poultry, shellfish, or egg in order to adjust the seasonings.

Do not eat steak tartare (raw hamburger), raw oysters, sushi, or ceviche (raw fish "cooked" in lime juice).

When marinating meat, seafood, or poultry, keep it refrigerated. Do not use a marinade that has been in contact with raw meat as a sauce for the cooked food without first bringing the marinade to a boil for at least one minute.

Never drink unpasteurized milk.

Thoroughly wash all fruits and vegetables with clean running water. Use a brush if necessary. Take special care to wash produce that will be eaten raw, such as lettuce and spinach. Discard outer leaves of leafy vegetables such as lettuce and cabbage.

Use oven mitts to remove hot items from the oven. This prevents nasty burns from the oven rack or the heating elements on electric ovens. Never use a wet mitt. The heat from pans or the stove can cause the water to steam and burn your hands.

Serving Food

Do not leave cooked meats or other perishable foods out for longer than two hours. Bacteria that can cause food poisoning grow quickly at room temperature.

Be careful of eating food from a buffet table. Do not eat the food unless the cold foods are cold and the hot foods are hot. At restaurants, be sure patrons are required to use new plates when returning to the buffet table for second helpings.

Use a clean plate or platter for cooked meat. Don't use the same plate the raw meat was on. Utensils and knives should be washed in between contact with raw and cooked foods.

Keep food at safe temperatures. Keep cold foods cold (at or below 40°F) and hot foods hot (at or above 140°F).

Leftovers should be reheated thoroughly before serving.

Cleaning

Wash counters and utensils with warm soapy water (use an antibacterial dishwashing liquid) after working with raw meat, poultry, or eggs.

Use the dishwasher to wash dishes whenever possible. The water temperature is higher and there is bleach in the dishwasher powder.

Sanitize cutting surfaces and countertops by washing with a solution of 2 teaspoons of household bleach in 1 quart of water. It is convenient to keep this solution in a spray bottle for easier cleaning. Rinse thoroughly with water. There are other commercial preparations available if you do not want to make your own cleaning compound. Check the label to choose an antibacterial solution.

When cleaning raw meat, poultry, seafood, and eggs from cooking and countertop surfaces, use paper towels instead of sponges or dishcloths. Discard the paper towels after use. This prevents contaminating your sponges and dishcloths with bacteria and it keeps them fresher by not having the odor of these raw foods embedded in their fibers.

Every night pour a small amount of bleach in the drain, especially if you have a garbage disposal, to eliminate odors and sanitize the drain. Avoid using the garbage disposal for grease, oil, and peels and trimmings from bananas, onions, bell peppers, and garlic. This will eliminate lingering odors and prevent drain blockage.

Take out the kitchen garbage on a regular basis, especially if there is any raw meat or meat juice. Egg shells, onions, and bell peppers also cause lingering odors so be sure they are removed from the kitchen, especially if you are suffering from nausea.

Change the dishcloth and dish towel daily. Wash dishcloths and dish towels with a small amount of bleach.

Place kitchen brushes and sponges in the dishwasher daily. Allow brushes and sponges to dry thoroughly.

When in doubt, throw it out.

Practical Cooking Hints
"The cooking lesson"

The recipes in this book use simple cooking methods. In the following section, we explain how to use some of these techniques or ingredients so that you can make great-tasting recipes.

If you are making a soup or sauce that requires sautéing of some of the ingredients (such as shallots, garlic, or onions) and has cream added to the mixture in the final stages of preparation, **be sure you sauté in butter.** The butterfat in cream and the butter from sautéing the vegetables are compatible and make an even smoother product. Vegetable oils and margarine do not mix well and can have an oily appearance.

51

When using flour for thickening in a recipe and it is not absolutely necessary that the sauce be ivory white, use browned flour for more flavor. To brown flour, pour enough flour in a nonstick frying pan to cover the bottom and carefully brown on low heat, stirring constantly. When the flour has browned, cool and store in an airtight container.

Nuts such as walnuts, almonds, hazelnuts, and pine nuts are more flavorful for eating, baking, and cooking if toasted. The natural oils come to the surface and give a more intense flavor, actually allowing use of less nuts in a recipe. Toast in a 300° oven with the nuts spread on a cookie sheet in one layer. Watch carefully and turn every five minutes. (Be careful, almonds brown fast. They go through three stages: not done, not done, burnt!) When the nuts are toasted, cool completely, place in airtight containers or freezer bags, and store in the freezer. Nuts stay fresher when stored in the freezer. Toast sesame and sunflower seeds before use. This can be done using a nonstick pan on the stove using low heat. Watch them carefully, since the small seeds can burn quickly.

To keep meat tender and flavorful with its own natural juices, do not salt and let the meat sit for long periods before cooking, as this causes the meat to release the juices. If you are cooking large pieces of meat or whole poultry, avoid poking with a fork. The flavorful juices are lost in the process. Turn with other utensils that do not puncture the surface. After meat or poultry has cooked in the oven, the juices have come to the surface in the heating process. Let the meat or poultry rest at room temperature after it has cooked before slicing so the natural juices can redistribute toward the center of the meat or poultry.

Mushrooms come in numerous varieties, not just the white buttons. Try using the brown mushrooms, Portobello mushrooms, or freeze-dried shitake mushrooms for a different flavor in cooking. A flavorful broth can be made by simmering mushroom pieces to the desired tenderness in the broth. The broth has now been infused with the mushroom flavor. Use the broth for cooking rice, Italian risotto, orzo, or very small pasta varieties.

Mushrooms should be cleaned very carefully. Rinse off the visible debris and pat dry. Do not peel mushrooms or soak in water (except freeze-dried varieties) or they will absorb the water like a sponge. When sautéing mushrooms in olive oil or butter, use a nonstick pan and have the oil or butter very hot before adding the mushrooms. The mushrooms will sizzle and "sing" as they sauté. Add a little salt and fresh ground pepper. Keep shaking the pan and turning the mushrooms. A small amount of liquid will be released. Serve immediately, including the "juices" that were released.

Many of the recipes in this book use **onions.** To prevent your eyes from tearing when cutting onions, put the onions in the refrigerator two hours before cutting. This prevents the volatile oils from being released when cutting the onions. These oils mix with the natural fluid in your eyes to produce mild sulfuric acid, which causes tearing.

Olive oil is a common ingredient in many ethnic cuisines including Italian, Greek, Spanish, Southern French (Provencal), and Middle Eastern. There are many brands and varieties available but this should not be intimidating. Olive oil is very versatile for cooking and seasoning. Extra virgin olive oil is the first press of the olives without using a heat process to extract the oil. It has a distinct fruity taste and a low smoking point so it should not be used in a heated cooking process. Extra virgin olive oil is used for topping pastas, dipping bread, marinating vegetables, and making salad dressing and hummus. The only other variety of olive oil that is needed for cooking is 100 percent olive oil which is the third press of the olives (virgin is the second press), using a heat process. It can sustain higher temperatures (but not as high as peanut, corn, or safflower oils) and thus is the olive oil of choice for sautéing vegetables, mushrooms, and meats and cooking fried eggs, omelets, and frittatas. When heating olive oil for sautéing, if you smell the olive oil, the temperature is too high!

Make your own yogurt cheese. Place plain or flavored yogurt in a large paper coffee filter that is inside a strainer. Suspend the strainer over a container to catch the liquid that drains from the yogurt. Cover the yogurt, and refrigerate for at least eight hours. Discard the liquid whey. The remaining yogurt can be used as a dip when mixed with other flavoring ingredients such as minced herbs, spices, sweeteners, mayonnaise, or sour cream. Use for dipping fruits, vegetables, chips, or crackers.

Use **plain yogurt** as a substitute for sour cream or butter in baked potatoes or mix with low-fat mayonnaise or low-fat sour cream to increase the flavor in creamy salads such as potato, cole slaw, macaroni, or ambrosia fruit.

When making soups, chili, pasta sauces, and casseroles that have vegetables added (onions, garlic, shallots, bell peppers, celery, carrots, etc.), the flavor will be greatly enhanced if the tasteless water from the vegetables is removed. Sauté and "sweat" the vegetables by heating a small amount of oil in a heavy frying pan, adding the vegetables, heating thoroughly at a high temperature, and then turning down the temperature to low. The water will "sweat" from the vegetables in about 5 to 10 minutes. Keep the heat low enough to prevent the vegetables from browning.

If you are making chicken salads and do not like to cook or handle raw chicken, an acceptable substitute is to buy fast-food fried chicken breasts. Remove the skin and bones and cut the meat into bite-size chunks or strips for the salad. The chicken meat is usually quite tender and moist from the cooking process used in the fast-food industry. Cooked, flavored, and cut chicken breasts are available in the poultry section of some grocery stores. These products are expensive but can help in a pinch.

When using **raisins** in recipes, try the golden variety. The raisins are not as dry and have a slightly sweeter taste. Raisins can be flavored and plumped in rum, brandy, or fruit juices. Use the liquid in the recipe or pour on cooked desserts such as custard and rice or bread pudding.

If a recipe calls for **candied citron,** substitute rum-soaked raisins, dried cranberries, cherries, apricots, pear, peaches, mission figs, mango, or papaya, and add orange or lemon zest. Dried fruits can be snipped into small pieces using kitchen shears.

Sun-dried tomatoes used in recipes can be easily cut into small pieces with kitchen shears.

Fresh basil becomes black when minced. If a recipe calls for fresh basil, roll the leaves together and make thin ribbon slices called a chiffonade.

Avocados can be ripened by putting in a brown paper bag with an apple. Check every day and be sure the avocado does not become mushy. An overly ripe avocado does not have a pleasant taste. Persimmons can also be ripened in the same manner.

53

Keep tomatoes at room temperature but out of direct sunlight.
The flavor of tomatoes is changed by storing them in the refrigerator.
Most tomatoes available in the store have little flavor unless the tomatoes are vine-ripened varieties. The lack of flavor comes from having the tomatoes picked before they are ripe so they can be transported with minimal bruising. Roma tomatoes are usually red and have the best flavor for a grocery store variety of tomato.

Do not store potatoes in the refrigerator. Store them in a dark, cool area. Refrigeration causes the starch to turn to sugar and alters the flavor of the product. If potatoes have turned green, cut away all the green parts. The green is caused by over exposure to light creating a slightly toxic chemical called solanine. It also makes the potato taste bitter.

54

When making muffins, mix gently and as little as possible to keep the muffins moist and light. The batter should look lumpy. Over-mixing will awaken the gluten in flour and toughen the muffins. There will be holes and tunnels in the muffins when over-mixed.

Many of the cream soups or sauces in this book use a **roux.** A roux is a thickener of equal parts of butter and flour cooked until the flour is no longer raw. The usual proportion of roux is 1 tablespoon butter to 1 tablespoon flour to thicken one cup of liquid. The longer the flour cooks, the darker the roux. Most white sauces are a combination of roux with milk added (Bechamel sauce). If stock is added, the sauce becomes a Veloute. Cajun cooking uses a brown roux.

There are two hints that are important to remember about roux. Be sure you cook it over low heat, stirring constantly with a wooden spoon until the flour is completely cooked or you will have a grainy, raw-tasting product, and it will not work as a thickener. This means at least 5 to 10 minutes of slow cooking. The other hint in making roux is to be sure the milk or stock added to the hot flour and butter mixture is cold or at room temperature to prevent lumps from forming.

If you are cooking with a water bath, open the oven door slowly. Steam produced from the water can easily burn your face if the oven door is opened quickly.

"Top it off"

Use **flavored bread crumbs** to top bland noodle dishes, vegetables, or casseroles, or add to meatloaf and meatball recipes. Mix dry bread crumbs with black pepper, garlic powder, Parmesan cheese, and basil. For creamed spinach and noodle dishes, omit the basil and add nutmeg to the bread crumbs. There are also commercial bread crumb mixes.

Make your own **"hotel butter"** by mincing garlic, salt, and parsley in a food processor and adding cold butter. Pulse until mixed. Use on baked potatoes, noodle dishes, rice dishes, toast, and bagels, and cooked fish, steaks, or chicken. Store tightly covered in the refrigerator.

Mix **cream cheese** with any of the following: blue cheese, minced chives, bell pepper or pimentos; chopped almonds and minced olives; finely chopped nuts, diced dates; dried cranberries and fine orange zest; walnuts and honey; cinnamon and raisins; pecans and maple syrup; orange marmalade, apricot, peach, raspberry, or strawberry jam; poppy seeds and lemon zest. Use as a topping for toast, bagels, crackers, celery, apple slices, or other fruits.

Make a **light dressing for fruit salad** using honey and orange juice. Add fresh mint leaves (when in season) to the salad.

55

Make a **light dressing for romaine lettuce salads** using extra virgin olive oil, lemon juice, garlic powder, and fresh ground black pepper. Top the salad with croutons and fresh grated Parmesan, Romano, or Asiago cheese.

Grate your own cheese such as Parmesan, Romano, and Asiago as needed for topping casseroles, pizza, garlic bread, pasta, soups, salads, and vegetables. There is more flavor in the freshly grated cheese than in commercial preparations sold in a can. Some grocery stores sell freshly grated cheese in the deli cheese section or will grate the cheese by request. Be sure the cheese is stored in an airtight container. The cheese grated in the store is done by a machine. If you handle the cheese with your fingers, you could contaminate the container of cheese with the mold that is present on hands. Use a spoon. This is also the rationale for not grating large quantities of any type of cheese by hand and storing in a container.

"Add spice to your life"

Make your own flavored sugar for adding to hot tea by mixing one cup of sugar with the zest of one lemon or orange and storing in an airtight container. Make your own vanilla sugar by adding one vanilla bean to two cups of sugar and storing for three days. Remove the vanilla bean. The bean can be reused if the sugar is brushed off and the bean is stored in an airtight container.

Add nutmeg to white sauces, white pasta, noodle dishes, or creamed vegetable dishes. **For extra flavor,** use freshly ground black pepper or grate nutmeg pods using a fine grater. Use finely minced fresh parsley instead of parsley flakes. Fresh herbs, such as basil, tarragon, and thyme are flavorful when added in the last few minutes of cooking. Dried herbs need to be added in the earlier stages of the cooking process.

Use **vanilla extract** instead of imitation vanilla for a better tasting product. When adding vanilla extract to cooked products (custards, sauces, and puddings), add it in the last few minutes of cooking so the aromatic flavor of the vanilla isn't destroyed.

The Recipes

Soups and Stews

Chicken Stock

Homemade chicken stock is crucial for delicious and nutritious cooking. The commercial preparation has sodium and fat, is very dilute, and cannot be reduced to make a thick sauce. Many of the recipes in this book use chicken stock. Chicken stock can be used for making soups, in place of water when cooking rice, when making dressings and stuffings, and for replacing oil or butter in recipes (white sauces for pasta, mashed potatoes, cooking vegetables, etc.). If you need to reduce the sodium in your diet, homemade stock is ideal because it does not have any salt added during the cooking process. It is made in large quantities and can be stored in the freezer for months.

60

If you would prefer to use a canned variety for convenience, Campbell's Healthy Request is low in sodium and has a good flavor. Some gourmet stores sell the reduced (most of the water removed) variety of stock that can be reconstituted and used in recipes.

Chicken Stock Recipe

5 pounds chicken backs, necks, or wings with all visible fat removed

2 pounds onions, peeled and cut into large chunks

1 pound carrots, peeled and cut into large pieces

5 stalks celery, cleaned and cut into large pieces (tops can be removed)

1 leek, cleaned and separated

3 cloves garlic, peeled

mushroom pieces (optional)

Bouquet Garni

In a piece of cheesecloth, tie:

1 bay leaf

1 teaspoon dried thyme or
  1 tablespoon fresh thyme

10 black peppercorns

2 whole cloves

8 sprigs fresh parsley

Place the chicken pieces in an 8- to 12-quart stockpot. Add the cut vegetables. Cover with enough cold water so that when you press the mixture down, there is at least 2 inches of water on top of the mixture. Bring the mixture to a boil. Skim off the white scum that forms. Turn the heat down to a very slow simmer. Add the bouquet garni. Let the mixture simmer for 2 to 3 hours, uncovered, skimming off fat during the cooking process.

Strain the mixture through a sieve into a large pot. Throw away the vegetables and the meat. (The chicken and vegetables are tasteless when they have been cooked for 3 hours.)

Make a cooling bath by putting ice cubes in the sink, adding cold water, and placing the pot in the sink. This will cool the stock faster. Change the ice and water after 15 minutes. Place the cooled pot in the refrigerator. Cool at least 12 hours.

Skim off the congealed fat and discard. The stock can be kept in the refrigerator for up to 5 days or stored in small plastic containers in the freezer for up to 6 months.

61

Bean and Barley Soup

The sausage adds a unique flavor to beans and barley.

1 medium onion, chopped
1 large carrot, diced
1 stalk celery, diced
2 cloves garlic, minced
1 tablespoon cooking oil
1/2 pound turkey sausage
15-ounce can white beans or
    light kidney beans, drained

1/2 cup pearl barley
1 1/2 cups water
1/4 teaspoon salt
1/2 teaspoon pepper
3 cups chicken broth
14-ounce can stewed tomatoes
1/2 teaspoon hot sauce (optional)

62

Cook onions, carrots, celery, and garlic in cooking oil in a large cooking pot until onions are translucent. Add turkey sausage and cook until light brown. Drain. Stir in remaining ingredients, and simmer uncovered about an hour. Adjust seasonings.

Serves 4

Nutritional Information per serving:
Calories: 450 • Fat: 14 gm. • Protein: 30 gm.
Carb.: 51 gm. • Cholesterol: 50 mg. • Fiber: very high

Black Bean Soup

A great favorite. Serve with toppings such as sour cream,
chopped tomatoes, salsa, avocado, or cilantro.

16 ounces dried black beans
2 cups chicken stock
1 bay leaf
1/2 teaspoon dried thyme
1 teaspoon black pepper
2 tablespoons vegetable oil
1 medium onion, diced
3 stalks celery, sliced

2 large carrots, peeled and sliced
1 medium red bell pepper, diced
2 cloves garlic, minced
1 pound lean ham, diced
1/4 cup sherry
2 teaspoons Worcestershire sauce
salt and pepper to taste

Wash beans and sort for stones and dirt. Put beans in a large soup pot
and cover with water (3 to 4 inches above beans). Bring to a boil. Boil
for 2 minutes. Remove from heat and let stand for 1 to 3 hours.

Pour off the soaking water. Add the chicken stock and enough water to
cover the beans with 2 inches of liquid. Add the bay leaf, thyme, and
black pepper. Bring to a boil, reduce heat, and simmer for 1 hour.

In a separate frying pan, heat the oil. Add onion, celery, carrots, red bell
pepper, and garlic. Cook on low heat until the onions are translucent.
Add vegetables and ham to the beans after they have cooked for 1 hour.
Simmer for another hour or until beans are soft.

Add the sherry and Worcestershire sauce. Adjust seasonings with salt
and pepper. Simmer for an additional 10 minutes. Serve with toppings
of your choice.

Serves 8

Nutritional Information per serving:
Calories: 325 • Fat: 7 gm. • Protein: 25 gm.
Carb.: 40 gm. • Cholesterol: 25 mg. • Fiber: very high

Butternut Squash Soup with Brandy

Cinnamon, nutmeg, and brandy—wow, is this good!

1 large butternut squash, peeled and cubed	2 tablespoons brandy
1 quart chicken broth	1 cup skim milk
2 tablespoons parsley, chopped	1 teaspoon molasses
1/8 teaspoon white pepper	1/8 teaspoon cinnamon
1/2 teaspoon marjoram	1/8 teaspoon nutmeg
	salt to taste

In a large saucepan, combine squash with broth, parsley, white pepper, and marjoram. Bring to a boil and simmer for 40 to 50 minutes or until squash is tender. Puree soup in a blender or food processor. Return soup to pan and add brandy. Stir. Add milk, molasses, and other seasonings. Heat thoroughly.

For an extra 60 calories per serving, substitute half and half for the skim milk.

Serves 4

Nutritional Information per serving:
Calories: 190 • Fat: 3 gm. • Protein: 15 gm.
Carb.: 24 gm. • Cholesterol: 4 mg. • Fiber: very low

Cauliflower Soup

....
Soft and smooth.
....

1 medium onion, diced
2 cloves garlic, minced
1 tablespoon butter or margarine
4 cups chicken stock
1 large cauliflower, chopped
2 large potatoes, peeled and
  chopped

1 bay leaf
1 cup milk
1/4 cup grated carrots
salt and pepper to taste
parsley for garnish

65

In a large saucepan, cook onion and garlic in butter until onions are translucent. Add chicken stock, cauliflower, potato, and bay leaf. Bring to a boil. Reduce heat and simmer for about 30 minutes or until vegetables are tender. Discard bay leaf. Process soup in a blender or food processor until smooth.

Return to saucepan. Stir in milk and grated carrots. Simmer 5 to 10 minutes or until carrots are tender. Adjust seasoning to taste. Garnish with parsley. Serve with fresh grated Parmesan cheese if desired.

Note: To prepare cauliflower, remove the tough core and dark green leaves. Soak the head in cold water for 10 minutes to remove dirt and bugs. Separate into florets, and chop.

For an extra 100 calories per serving, substitute heavy cream for the milk. For an extra 50 calories per serving, add 2 tablespoons Parmesan cheese to each bowl of soup.

Serves 6

Nutritional Information per serving:
Calories: 100 • Fat: 4 gm. • Protein: 6 gm.
Carb.: 9 gm. • Cholesterol: 10 mg. • Fiber: low

Cheesy Broccoli Soup

Broccoli cheese soup—vitamin rich.

1 medium onion, finely chopped
1 stalk celery, diced
1 cup carrots, diced
10 ounces fresh or frozen
  broccoli, chopped
2 tablespoons butter or margarine
4 tablespoons flour

4 cups chicken broth
4 cups milk
8 ounces fat-free processed
  American cheese
1/4 teaspoon white pepper
1/4 teaspoon nutmeg
salt to taste

In a heavy saucepan, cook onion, celery, carrots, and broccoli in butter until tender. Stir in flour and cook for 5 minutes, stirring constantly. Add chicken broth, stirring constantly until it thickens. Add milk and cheese. Add pepper, nutmeg, and salt. Stir. Heat until cheese melts. Adjust seasonings to taste.

For an extra 230 calories per serving, substitute half and half for the milk and use regular cheese.

Serves 8

Nutritional Information per serving:
Calories: 240 • Fat: 11 gm. • Protein: 20 gm.
Carb.: 14 gm. • Cholesterol: 40 mg. • Fiber: low

Chicken Vegetable Soup

An old fashioned favorite.

4 chicken breast halves
1 large onion, chopped
1 tablespoon cooking oil
1 quart chicken broth
1/2 teaspoon dried thyme
1 bay leaf
3 sprigs parsley

2 stalks celery, chopped
4 large carrots, peeled and chopped
2 parsnips, peeled and sliced (optional)
2 cups mushrooms, sliced (optional)
4 large potatoes, cubed
salt and pepper to taste

67

In a heavy soup pot, brown chicken breasts and onions in oil. Drain any excess oil. Add chicken broth and enough water to cover chicken. Add thyme, bay leaf, and parsley. Bring to a boil and then simmer until chicken is tender (about 1 hour).

Remove chicken from broth. Remove the lean meat from the bones, discarding the skin, fat, and bones. Put meat back into broth. Add all remaining ingredients and cook until vegetables are tender. Adjust seasonings. Add more broth if too thick.

Clear soup option: For a clear soup, pour soup through a strainer. Use the vegetables and meat for other recipes.

Pureed soup option: For a pureed soup, process soup in a food processor or blender until smooth.

Serves 8

Nutritional Information per serving:
Calories: 240 • Fat: 10 gm. • Protein: 23 gm.
Carb.: 15 gm. • Cholesterol: 50 mg. • Fiber: medium

Chunky Gazpacho Garden Soup

Cold summer soup with a zesty flavor.

6 tomatoes, diced
1 clove garlic, minced
1 large cucumber, peeled and chopped
10 green onions, diced
1 tablespoon olive oil
1 tablespoon cider vinegar

46 ounces V-8 vegetable juice or tomato juice
2 teaspoons Worcestershire sauce
1 tablespoon lemon juice
1 teaspoon lime juice
6 dashes Tabasco sauce
salt and pepper

Combine all ingredients in a large bowl. Cover tightly and refrigerate at least 8 hours. The soup will thicken slightly from the vegetable pectin. Serve cold.

Serves 8

Nutritional Information per serving:
Calories: 140 • Fat: 2 gm. • Protein: 5 gm.
Carb.: 26 gm. • Cholesterol: 0 • Fiber high

Corn and Crab Bisque

Super elegant flavor.

1 medium onion, chopped
4 tablespoons butter or margarine
4 tablespoons flour
3 cups chicken stock
2 cups milk
1/2 teaspoon dry mustard
2 teaspoons Worcestershire sauce

1/4 teaspoon Tabasco sauce
1/2 teaspoon white pepper
1 pound crab surimi seafood chunks
3 cups frozen corn
1/4 cup sherry
salt to taste

69

In a heavy pan, cook onions in butter over low heat until they are translucent. Stir in flour and cook for 5 minutes, stirring constantly. Add stock and milk. Bring to a boil, stirring continually until mixture thickens. Reduce heat. Add seasonings, crab, and corn, and simmer about 15 minutes. Add sherry and adjust seasonings.

For an extra 65 calories per serving, substitute half and half for the milk. For an extra 225 calories per serving, substitute heavy cream for the milk.

Serves 6

Nutritional Information per serving:
Calories: 360 • Fat: 13 gm. • Protein: 24 gm.
Carb.: 37 gm. • Cholesterol: 55 mg. • Fiber: low

Corn Chowder

Traditional corn chowder uses bacon. In order to decrease the odor in the kitchen for those who may not tolerate the smell of bacon frying, lean ham has been substituted. For an extra spicy soup, pass the Tabasco or your favorite hot sauce.

1 medium onion, chopped
2 stalks celery, tops removed, sliced
2 tablespoons butter or margarine
2 tablespoons flour
4 cups chicken stock
2 medium potatoes, peeled
  and cubed
3/4 cup milk
1/4 cup heavy cream (optional)

1 cup lean ham, diced
4 cups frozen corn
1 teaspoon freshly ground pepper
1 medium red bell pepper, diced
salt to taste
2 tablespoons parsley, minced
pinch red pepper flakes
parsley for garnish
croutons for garnish

Over low heat in a large soup pot, cook onions and celery in butter until onions are translucent. Add flour and cook on low heat, stirring constantly for 5 minutes. Add chicken stock and potatoes. Keep the pot at a low simmer until the potatoes are just tender. Stir occasionally. Add milk, cream, ham, corn, and pepper. Cook for 5 minutes. Add red bell pepper, salt, parsley, and red pepper flakes. Cook for an additional 5 minutes over low heat. Serve in hot bowls garnished with additional parsley and croutons.

Serves 6

Nutritional Information per serving:
Calories: 300 • Fat: 12 gm. • Protein: 14 gm.
Carb.: 35 gm. • Cholesterol: 40 mg. • Fiber: high

Cream of Mushroom Soup with Brandy

The nutmeg and brandy warm the heart.

1 large onion, chopped
2 pounds fresh mushrooms, sliced
1 clove garlic, minced
4 tablespoons butter or margarine
3 tablespoons flour
4 cups chicken broth

3 cups milk
1/4 teaspoon white pepper
1/4 teaspoon nutmeg
salt to taste
2 tablespoons brandy

In a large saucepan, cook onions, mushrooms, and garlic in butter until tender. Add flour and cook, stirring constantly, for at least 5 minutes. Add broth and bring to a boil, stirring continually until mixture thickens. Add milk and seasonings. Heat to simmering. Stir in brandy just before serving.

For an extra 60 calories per serving, substitute half and half for the milk.

Serves 8

Nutritional Information per serving:
Calories: 200 • Fat: 10 gm. • Protein: 12 gm.
Carb.: 14 gm. • Cholesterol: 30 mg. • Fiber: low

Easy Chili

Great chili—just as good as long, complicated
recipes and ready in less than an hour.

1 pound ground beef	30-ounce can kidney beans
1 large onion, chopped	2 teaspoons chili powder
1/2 teaspoon salt	1 teaspoon cumin
1/2 teaspoon pepper	1/2 teaspoon oregano flakes
15-ounce can chopped tomatoes	2 fresh jalapeño chiles, minced
15-ounce can tomato sauce	(optional)

72

In a large heavy soup pan, brown meat and onion. Drain well. Season
with salt and pepper. Add tomatoes, tomato sauce, kidney beans, chili
powder, cumin, oregano, and chiles. Bring to a boil. Reduce heat and
simmer uncovered for about 30 minutes.

Note: For a thinner chili, substitute a large 46-ounce can of tomato juice
for the 15-ounce can of tomatoes and 8-ounce can of tomato sauce in
this recipe.

Serves 6

Nutritional Information per serving:
Calories: 380 • Fat: 21 gm. • Protein: 22 gm.
Carb.: 28 gm. • Cholesterol: 65 mg. • Fiber: low

Fresh Peach Soup

So refreshing!

3 cups diced honeydew melon
1/2 cup fresh orange juice
1/2 cup low-fat vanilla yogurt
1 tablespoon honey

2 teaspoons fresh lime juice
2 cups diced peeled peaches
   (1 1/2 pounds)
1 cup blueberries, fresh or frozen

Place melon, orange juice, yogurt, honey, and lime juice in a food processor. Process until smooth. Combine melon mixture with diced peaches and blueberries in a bowl. Stir well. Cover and chill before serving.

73

Serves 6

Nutritional Information per serving:
Calories: 85 • Fat: 0 • Protein 2 gm.
Carb.: 20 gm. • Cholesterol: 0 • Fiber low

Lentil, Tomato, and Spinach Soup

This soup is a real flavor treat and it provides lots of nutrients and fiber. To increase the calories and protein, add diced lean ham and small cooked pasta to the soup. The soup can also be served over rice.

1 pound dried lentils
4 cups chicken stock
1 bay leaf
1/2 teaspoon thyme
1 medium onion, diced
2 large carrots, peeled and diced
2 stalks celery, tops removed, diced
2 tablespoons olive oil
2 cloves garlic, minced
14-ounce can tomatoes, chopped
8 ounces frozen spinach, thawed and squeezed dry

1 teaspoon dried basil
1 teaspoon Angostura bitters (optional)
1 teaspoon freshly ground black pepper
salt to taste
2 tablespoons red wine vinegar or lemon juice
1/2 cup freshly grated Parmesan cheese
fresh ground pepper

74

Wash lentils and check for small stones. Place lentils in a large soup pot. Add chicken stock. Add additional water to cover lentils with at least 2 inches of liquid. Bring lentils to a boil, then reduce heat and simmer. Add bay leaf and thyme. While lentils are slowly simmering, cook the onions, carrots, and celery in olive oil until onions are translucent. Do not brown the vegetables. Add garlic near the end of the cooking process. Add the cooked vegetables, tomatoes, spinach, basil, bitters, black pepper, and salt to the lentils. Simmer until lentils are soft but not mushy.

Near the end of the cooking process, add the vinegar or lemon juice. If necessary, adjust the seasonings with salt and pepper. Remove the bay leaf. Serve in warmed bowls garnished with freshly grated Parmesan cheese and fresh ground pepper.

Serves 6

Nutritional Information per serving:
Calories: 365 • Fat: 4 gm. • Protein: 30 gm.
Carb.: 53 gm. • Cholesterol: 5 mg. • Fiber: very high

Minestrone Soup

1 medium onion, diced
2 large carrots, peeled and diced
2 stalks celery, diced
2 cloves garlic, minced
2 tablespoons olive oil
32 ounces beef broth
15-ounce can Italian style
    tomatoes, undrained,
    coarsely chopped
1 teaspoon dried basil

1 teaspoon dried oregano
3 tablespoons fresh parsley, minced
1/2 cup ditalini pasta, uncooked
15-ounce can kidney beans, red
    or white
2 medium zucchini, diced
salt and pepper to taste
1/2 cup freshly grated Parmesan
    cheese

In a large soup pot, cook onions, carrots, celery, and garlic in olive oil until onions are translucent. Add beef broth, tomatoes, basil, oregano, and parsley. Cook for 30 minutes. Add the pasta, beans, and zucchini. Cook for an additional 8 to 10 minutes until the pasta is cooked. Season with salt and pepper. Garnish each bowl with freshly grated Parmesan cheese.

For an extra 80 calories per serving, add an extra 2 tablespoons Parmesan cheese per bowl.

Serves 4

Nutritional Information per serving:
Calories: 375 • Fat: 13 gm. • Protein: 22 gm.
Carb.: 41 gm. • Cholesterol: 10 mg. • Fiber: very high

Mushroom, Green Onion, and Leek Soup

1/4 pound butter or margarine

2 bunches green onions, cleaned and coarsely chopped

2 medium leeks, white parts only, coarsely chopped

2 cloves garlic, sliced

1/2 teaspoon salt

1/4 teaspoon white pepper

1/2 teaspoon black pepper

1/4 teaspoon cayenne pepper (optional)

4 tablespoons flour

6 cups chicken stock

1 pound fresh brown crimini or white mushrooms, cleaned, bottoms trimmed, coarsely chopped

1 teaspoon lemon rind, grated

1/4 cup white wine

1/2 cup grated carrots

salt and freshly ground pepper to taste

In a large soup pot, melt butter. Add green onions, leeks, and garlic. Cook on low heat for 10 minutes. Add salt, white pepper, black pepper, and cayenne pepper. Stir. Add the flour and cook slowly for 5 minutes. Add the chicken stock and bring to a boil, whisking continually. Reduce heat; add mushrooms, and cook for 8 minutes. Add lemon rind and white wine. Cook for an additional 5 minutes. Adjust seasonings with salt and pepper. Puree soup in batches. Garnish each serving with grated carrots.

For an extra 25 calories per serving, use an additional 2 tablespoons of butter in the recipe.

Serves 8

Nutritional Information per serving:
Calories: 200 • Fat: 13 gm. • Protein: 7 gm.
Carb.: 14 gm. • Cholesterol 30 mg. • Fiber: low

Pasta and Bean Soup (Pasta e fagioli)

Serve this soup with crunchy garlic bread
and a salad for a complete meal.

2 tablespoons olive oil
1 medium onion, diced
2 stalks celery, tops removed, sliced
2 large carrots, peeled and sliced
2 cloves garlic, minced
4 cups chicken stock
1/4 cup red wine
15-ounce can cannellini, Great Northern, or white beans, drained
15-ounce can red kidney beans, drained

14-ounce can chopped tomatoes
1 bay leaf
1 teaspoon dried basil
1/2 teaspoon oregano
1/2 cup dried ditalini or small shell pasta
1/4 cup parsley, chopped
salt and freshly ground pepper to taste
1 cup freshly grated Parmesan cheese

In a large soup pot, heat the olive oil. Add onions, celery, and carrots. Cook over low heat for 5 to 7 minutes. Add garlic and cook an additional 3 minutes. Do not brown any of the vegetables. The celery and carrots will still be firm. Add stock, wine, beans, tomatoes, bay leaf, basil, and oregano. Simmer for 10 minutes. Add more stock or water if the mixture is too thick. Add pasta and parsley and cook until the pasta is just cooked. Adjust the seasonings with salt and pepper. Remove from heat. Remove the bay leaf. Let the soup stand for 10 minutes. Adjust seasonings if necessary. Serve in warmed pasta bowls with generous amount of freshly grated Parmesan cheese.

To add 160 extra calories per serving, add 1/2 pound cooked lean ground beef and an extra 1 cup grated Parmesan cheese to the recipe.

Serves 6

Nutritional Information per serving:
Calories: 350 • Fat: 11 gm. • Protein: 23 gm.
Carb.: 39 gm. • Cholesterol: 10 mg. • Fiber: very high

Potato and Bean Soup

Hearty potato soup.

1 medium onion, chopped
1 tablespoon cooking oil
4 cups chicken stock
3 medium potatoes, cut in
　1/2 inch cubes
15-ounce can Great Northern
　beans, drained

15-ounce can red kidney beans,
　drained
8-ounce can tomato sauce
1/2 teaspoon dried basil leaves
1/2 teaspoon dried oregano leaves
salt and freshly ground pepper to
　taste

In a small frying pan, cook onions in oil until translucent. In a large saucepan, combine onions with all remaining ingredients. Simmer for 30 to 40 minutes or until potatoes are tender. Adjust seasonings to taste.

Serves 8

Nutritional Information per serving:
Calories: 450 • Fat: 4 gm. • Protein: 30 gm.
Carb.: 75 gm. • Cholesterol: 5 mg. • Fiber: very high

Pumpkin Soup

Wow—loaded with vitamin A!

1 medium onion, finely chopped
2 tablespoons butter or margarine
2 tablespoons flour
4 cups chicken stock
8-ounce can pumpkin
1 teaspoon lemon juice

1/2 teaspoon pepper
1/4 teaspoon nutmeg
1/4 teaspoon ginger
1 cup evaporated skim milk
lemon slices for garnish

In a large soup pot, cook onions in butter until translucent. Add flour and cook, stirring constantly, for 5 minutes over low heat. Add chicken stock and stir continually until mixture boils and thickens. Stir in remaining ingredients. Simmer 10 minutes. Adjust seasonings to taste. Garnish each bowl with a slice of lemon.

For an extra 100 calories per serving, substitute heavy cream for the evaporated skim milk.

79

Serves 6

Nutritional Information per serving:
Calories: 155 • Fat: 6 gm. • Protein: 12 gm.
Carb.: 14 gm. • Cholesterol: 15 mg. • Fiber: low

Split Pea Soup

What a great meal to make ahead. Make an
extra large batch and freeze in small containers.

3 cups dry green split peas
1 large onion, chopped
3 stalks celery, chopped
2 large carrots, peeled and chopped
1 shallot clove, minced
2 garlic cloves, minced
1 tablespoon cooking oil

2 large potatoes, peeled and
  chopped (optional)
2 cups chicken stock
1 teaspoon thyme
1 bay leaf
1 pound lean ham, diced
salt and freshly ground pepper to
  taste

80

Wash peas in a colander. Place peas in a large cooking pot and cover
with water. Bring to a boil. Reduce heat and simmer for 1 to 2 hours
until peas are tender and mushy. (Do not add any salt, salty foods, or
high-acid foods before the peas are soft. Salt and acid ingredients will
prevent the peas from becoming soft.) In a large frying pan, cook
chopped onions, celery, carrots, shallots, and garlic in oil until onions
are translucent.

After peas are soft, add onion mixture, potatoes, chicken stock, thyme,
bay leaf, and ham. Simmer until vegetables are tender and soup has
thickened. Stir occasionally and add extra water or chicken broth if
soup gets too thick. Adjust seasoning with salt and pepper. Remove bay
leaf.

Optional: For a very smooth consistency, process soup in a food
processor or blender.

Serves 8

Nutritional Information per serving:
Calories: 370 • Fat: 5 gm. • Protein: 30 gm.
Carb.: 52 gm. • Cholesterol: 25 mg. • Fiber: very high

Vegetable Soup

Add any combination of vegetables to suit your taste.

1 large onion, chopped
1 tablespoon butter or margarine
1 sweet potato, peeled and diced
2 white potatoes, peeled and diced
2 large carrots, peeled and diced
2 large zucchini, sliced

1 cup green beans
4–6 cups chicken or beef broth
2 cups broccoli florets, chopped
1 cup green peas
1/4 teaspoon paprika
salt and pepper to taste

In a frying pan, cook onions in butter until translucent. In a large soup pot, combine onions with sweet potatoes, white potatoes, carrots, zucchini, and beans. Add broth.

81

Bring to a boil. Reduce heat and simmer for about 30 minutes. Add broccoli, peas, and paprika 10 minutes before serving. Season to taste. The soup can be pureed in a blender or food processor if desired.

Serves 8

Nutritional Information per serving:
Calories: 215 • Fat: 3 gm. • Protein: 15 gm.
Carb.: 32 gm. • Cholesterol: 5 mg. • Fiber: very high

White Bean Soup

A hearty meal.

1 pound Great Northern beans	2 tablespoons olive oil
1 onion, chopped	1 pound lean ham, cubed
2 stalks celery, diced	1 bay leaf
2 carrots, peeled and diced	1 teaspoon dried thyme
1 clove garlic, minced	salt and freshly ground pepper

Sort and wash beans. Place in a large cooking pot. Cover with water. Bring to a boil, then turn off heat. Let stand for 1 to 2 hours.

Pour off water and replace with fresh water. In a large frying pan, cook onions, celery, carrots, and garlic in oil until onions are translucent. Add vegetable mixture to the beans and water. Add ham. Add bay leaf and thyme. Bring to a boil. Reduce heat and simmer for about 2 hours or until beans are tender and soup has thickened. Stir occasionally.

Add salt and pepper to taste. Remove bay leaf. Additional herbs may be added to suit your taste. To make a thicker soup, place 2 cups of bean mixture in a blender or food processor. Process until smooth. Return puree to pan. If desired, puree all of the soup.

Serves 6

Nutritional Information per serving:
Calories: 415 • Fat: 9 gm. • Protein: 32 gm.
Carb.: 52 gm. • Cholesterol: 35 mg. • Fiber: very high

Wild Rice Soup

Delicate and elegant.

1 small onion, minced	1/2 cup grated carrots
1 tablespoon butter or margarine	1 cup half and half
2 tablespoons flour	1 tablespoon sherry
4 cups chicken stock	salt and pepper to taste
2 cups cooked wild rice	1/4 cup slivered almonds, toasted

Cook onions in butter in a heavy saucepan until onions are translucent. Stir in flour and cook over low heat, stirring constantly at least 5 minutes. Add chicken stock and bring to a boil, stirring continually. Add cooked wild rice and grated carrots. Bring to a boil. Reduce heat and cook for 10 minutes or until carrots are tender. Add half and half and heat thoroughly. Add sherry and seasonings to taste. Serve with toasted almonds on top.

83

Serves 6

Nutritional Information per serving:
Calories: 230 • Fat: 11 gm. • Protein: 12 gm.
Carb.: 20 gm. • Cholesterol: 20 mg. • Fiber: low

Salads

Apple Turkey Salad

Honey mustard with apples, raisins, and turkey.

1/2 cup fat-free mayonnaise
1 teaspoon Dijon mustard
2 teaspoons honey
2 teaspoons lemon juice
1/8 teaspoon nutmeg
2 cups baked turkey breast, cubed

2 large apples, cored and diced
2 stalks celery, diced
1 cup golden raisins
2 tablespoons sesame seeds,
  toasted

In a large bowl, combine mayonnaise, mustard, honey, lemon juice, and nutmeg. Stir in turkey, apples, celery, and raisins. Sprinkle with toasted sesame seeds right before serving.

Note: Fresh grapes can be substituted for the raisins.

For an extra 170 calories per serving, use regular mayonnaise.

Serves 4

Nutritional Information per serving:
Calories: 375 • Fat: 10 gm. • Protein: 26 gm.
Carb.: 46 gm. • Cholesterol: 70 mg. • Fiber: medium

Asparagus with Honey Mustard Vinaigrette

One of those special spring salads. A sweet-tart vinaigrette served over tender asparagus spears.

2 pounds thin fresh asparagus spears

Vinaigrette

1/4 cup extra virgin olive oil

1 tablespoon lemon or orange juice

1 teaspoon white wine vinegar

1 tablespoon honey mustard

1/2 teaspoon lemon or orange rind, finely grated

1/2 teaspoon freshly ground pepper

1/4 cup finely chopped toasted almonds (optional)

To make the vinaigrette, whisk all the ingredients together in a small bowl. The vinaigrette may be stored for up to one week in the refrigerator. Let the vinaigrette warm to room temperature before drizzling over cooked asparagus spears.

Bend the asparagus stalks and break off the woody ends. Soak in cold water for a few minutes. Bring a large pot of water to boil. Add 1 teaspoon salt to the boiling water. Have a large pan of ice water ready. Toss the asparagus spears in the boiling salted water. Cook until just tender (3 to 7 minutes). Quickly remove the spears from the boiling water with tongs and drop in the ice water to stop the cooking process. Drain, then pat dry. Arrange asparagus spears on a large platter and drizzle with the vinaigrette. Sprinkle with toasted almonds.

Note: The cooked asparagus spears can be wrapped in paper towels, placed in a plastic bag, and stored for three days in the refrigerator.

Serves 4

Nutritional Information per serving:
Calories: 175 • Fat: 16 gm. • Protein: 4 gm.
Carb.: 7 gm. • Cholesterol: 0 • Fiber: medium

Banana Apple Salad

Crunchy fruit salad with a citrus-honey dressing.

1 large banana, sliced
3/4 cup raisins
1/2 cup celery, chopped

2 large apples, cored and diced
1/3 cup toasted walnuts

Dressing

3 ounces orange juice, frozen
concentrate
2 tablespoons honey

1 tablespoon apple cider vinegar
1 teaspoon poppy seeds

Combine banana, raisins, celery, and apples in serving dish. Shake together dressing ingredients in a small jar. Pour dressing over salad and toss. Top with toasted walnuts.

For an extra 50 calories per serving, add 2 tablespoons salad oil to the dressing.

Serves 4

Nutritional Information per serving:
Calories: 230 • Fat: 2 gm. • Protein: 2 gm.
Carb.: 52 gm. • Cholesterol: 0 • Fiber: high

Black Bean Salad

Colorful, zesty, high protein, and high fiber salad.

30-ounce can black beans, drained

1/2 medium red onion, finely diced

1/2 medium red pepper, diced

1 cup chopped Roma tomatoes

2 cloves garlic, finely minced

1 small jalapeño chile, finely minced

4 tablespoons extra virgin olive oil

1 tablespoon lime juice

salt and freshly ground pepper to taste

1/2 cup fresh cilantro, chopped

89

In a large bowl, mix the beans with onions, peppers, tomatoes, garlic, and jalapeño chile. In a separate bowl, whisk the olive oil and lime juice together. Pour over the bean mixture and gently mix. Adjust the seasonings with salt and pepper. Refrigerate for at least 4 hours. Add cilantro right before serving.

Serves 6

Nutritional Information per serving:
Calories: 290 • Fat: 10 gm. • Protein: 13 gm.
Carb.: 37 gm. • Cholesterol: 0 • Fiber: very high

Broccoli Sunflower Salad

This is a winning combination of flavors.

5 cups broccoli florets
1/2 cup raisins
1/4 small red onion, sliced

10 strips bacon, fried and
crumbled
1 cup toasted sunflower seeds

Dressing

2 tablespoons sugar
1 cup fat-free mayonnaise

3 tablespoons white wine vinegar

Blanch broccoli florets in a pan of boiling salted water for 1 minute. Chill quickly under cold running water. Drain and pat dry. In a large bowl, combine broccoli, raisins, onions, bacon, and sunflower seeds. Mix together the dressing ingredients in a small jar.

Pour dressing over salad and toss. Refrigerate for several hours before serving.

For an extra 240 calories per serving, use regular mayonnaise. Sprinkle with grated cheese for extra protein.

Serves 6

Nutritional Information per serving:
Calories: 265 • Fat: 12 gm. • Protein: 10 gm.
Carb.: 29 gm. • Cholesterol: 10 mg. • Fiber: high

Corn Salsa Salad

Crunchy summer vegetables in a light lime
marinade dressing go well with grilled meats.

1 pound frozen corn, thawed, or
   15-ounce can vacuum packed
   niblet corn
1/2 pound fresh tomatoes,
   chopped and drained
1 bunch scallions, thinly sliced
1 medium red bell pepper,
   diced, seeds removed
2 stalks celery, sliced
1/2 small red onion, diced
1 small jalapeño chile, minced
   (optional)

1 clove garlic, minced
1/2 cup fresh cilantro, chopped
2 tablespoons fresh lime juice
3 tablespoons olive oil
1/2 teaspoon salt
freshly ground pepper to taste
dash cayenne pepper (optional)
dash Tabasco sauce (optional)
Garnish options: sour cream and
   diced avocado

91

In a large bowl, mix the vegetables, jalapeño chile, garlic, and cilantro.
In a small bowl, whisk lime juice, olive oil, salt, pepper, and Tabasco
sauce together. Pour over the vegetables. Refrigerate for at least 30 minutes, stirring after 15 minutes. Serve with sour cream and avocado garnish, if desired. Tortilla chips make a crunchy base for the salad.

Serves 6

Nutritional Information per serving:
Calories: 160 • Fat: 7 gm. • Protein: 3 gm.
Carb.: 21 gm. • Cholesterol: 0 • Fiber: medium

Crunchy Pea Salad

A great crisp taste combination.

2 cups frozen peas
1 cup celery, finely chopped

8-ounce can water chestnuts,
drained and diced

Dressing

1/2 cup fat-free sour cream
1 teaspoon Beau Monde seasoning
or 1/2 teaspoon lemon pepper

1 tablespoon soy sauce

92

1/2 cup dry roasted peanuts

In a large bowl, combine peas, celery, and water chestnuts. Set aside. In a small bowl, combine sour cream, seasoning, and soy sauce. Stir dressing into vegetables. Toss until blended. Cover and refrigerate for several hours or overnight. When ready to serve, add peanuts.

For an extra 130 calories per serving, use regular sour cream and add an extra 1/2 cup of peanuts to the recipe.

Serves 4

Nutritional Information per serving:
Calories: 240 • Fat: 10 gm. • Protein: 10 gm.
Carb.: 27 gm. • Cholesterol: 5 mg. • Fiber: high

Donna's Healthy Potato Salad

This recipe is a real surprise. Well worth a try!
This great potato salad is low in fat and calories but
tastes just like the regular high-calorie potato salad.

2 pounds red potatoes
1 medium red onion, diced
1/2 cup celery, diced
3 tablespoons fat-free
  French dressing
1/2 cup fat-free mayonnaise

1/2 tablespoon Durkees Famous
  Sauce
1 tablespoon Dijon mustard
dash Tabasco sauce
1/4 teaspoon white pepper
salt to taste

93

In a saucepan, boil potatoes just until fork tender. (Do not overcook.)
Peel and dice.

In a large bowl, combine warm potatoes with onions and celery. Gently
stir French dressing into potatoes and marinate for an hour at room temperature. Set aside. In a small bowl, combine mayonnaise, Durkees
sauce, mustard, Tabasco, white pepper, and salt. Taste the dressing and
add more mustard or seasonings to suit your taste. Combine dressing
with potatoes. Refrigerate until ready to serve.

Serves 5

Nutritional Information per serving:
Calories: 140 • Fat: 0 • Protein: 4 gm.
Carb.: 30 gm. • Cholesterol: 0 • Fiber: medium

Gorgeous Fruit Salad

A colorful, beautiful salad that is refreshing when strawberries
are in season. Serve as a salad with toasted egg bread (challah or
brioche) or as a dessert with delicate cookies.

1/2 whole fresh pineapple,
   peeled and cubed
4 kiwifruit, peeled and sliced
10-ounce can mandarin oranges,
   drained
2 large Granny Smith apples,
   peeled and diced
1/2 cup orange juice

1 tablespoon honey
1 teaspoon Grand Marnier
1 pound fresh strawberries, hulled
   and sliced in half
1/4 cup mint leaves
1/2 cup toasted coconut, sesame
   seeds, or sunflower seeds

In a large bowl, combine pineapple, kiwis, mandarin oranges, and
apples. In a small bowl mix the orange juice, honey, and Grand Marnier.
Pour over the fruit and toss very gently. Refrigerate for at least 2 hours
tightly covered with plastic wrap.

Just before serving, add the strawberries and mint leaves. Toss gently.
Top with toasted coconut, sesame seeds, or sunflower seeds.

Serves 8

Nutritional Information per serving:
Calories: 120 • Fat: 1 gm. • Protein: 2 gm.
Carb.: 26 gm. • Cholesterol: 0 • Fiber: high

Green Beans and
Toasted Almond Salad

1 pound fresh green beans,
  rinsed, tough strings removed,
  cut into 2-inch pieces
1 cup sliced scallions or 1/2 red
  onion, thinly sliced
1/4 red bell pepper, diced
2 cloves garlic, minced

1/4 cup extra virgin olive oil
juice of 1 lemon
1 tablespoon white wine vinegar
salt and freshly ground black pepper
  to taste
1 cup toasted almonds, chopped

95

Blanch green beans in boiling salted water until crisp tender. Drain. In a medium bowl, combine the green beans, scallions or red onion, pepper, and garlic. Drizzle olive oil over vegetables and toss. Add lemon juice, vinegar, black pepper, and salt. Toss gently to mix. Refrigerate for at least 2 hours. Right before serving, add toasted almonds.

To add more calories, toss 2 boiled, sliced potatoes in the salad before refrigerating.

Serves 4

Nutritional Information per serving:
Calories: 275 • Fat: 20 gm. • Protein: 5 gm.
Carb.: 19 gm. • Cholesterol: 0 • Fiber: high

Jicama Orange Salad

A refreshing crunchy and sweet salad. Serve with
a bean dish or chili. Low in calories and easy to make.

1 pound jicama, peeled and diced
2 medium navel oranges, peeled
    and cut in chunks
1/2 cup chopped cilantro
2 tablespoons lime juice

1/4 teaspoon salt
1 fresh jalapeño chile, minced
    (optional)
freshly ground pepper to taste

96

Mix all ingredients together. Cover and chill 1 hour before serving.

Serves 4

Nutritional Information per serving:
Calories: 75 • Fat: 0 • Protein: 2 gm.
Carb.: 17 gm. • Cholesterol: 0 • Fiber: high

Mediterranean Tuna, Bean, and Pasta Salad

Memories of that summer picnic.

12 ounces small pasta shells
1 pound green beans, fresh
    or frozen
12-ounce can solid white
    albacore tuna in water, drained
1/2 cup black pitted olives

1/4 cup extra virgin olive oil
2 tablespoons white wine vinegar
    or lemon juice
3 cloves garlic, minced
1 teaspoon tarragon
salt and pepper to taste

97

In a large saucepan, cook pasta in boiling water just until tender. Drain. Set aside. In a large saucepan, cook green beans until tender. Drain. In a large bowl, combine cooked pasta, beans, tuna, and olives. Set aside. In a small jar, combine the olive oil with remaining ingredients. Stir dressing into pasta mixture. Serve warm or chilled.

For an extra 100 calories per serving, add 8 ounces of feta cheese to the recipe.

Serves 6

Nutritional Information per serving:
Calories: 400 • Fat: 11 gm. • Protein: 23 gm.
Carb.: 52 gm. • Cholesterol: 15 mg. • Fiber: medium

Orange Cream Fruit Salad

Creamy sweet orange flavor on fresh or canned
fruits. Choose any fruit of your choice.

1 cup pineapple tidbits, drained
1 cup canned peaches, drained
1 cup mandarin oranges, drained
1 large apple, sliced
1 package instant vanilla pudding
  mix

1 1/2 cups skim milk
1/3 cup frozen orange juice
  concentrate, thawed
1/3 cup fat-free sour cream
1 medium firm banana, sliced

In a large salad bowl, combine pineapple, peaches, oranges, and apples.
Set aside.

In a small bowl, use an electric mixer to beat together pudding mix,
milk, and orange juice concentrate. Stir in sour cream and mix well. Add
dressing to the fruit and stir gently to coat. Refrigerate until ready to
serve. Add banana slices right before serving.

To add 50 calories per serving, use regular sour cream.

Serves 6

Nutritional Information per serving:
Calories: 200 • Fat: 0 • Protein: 4 gm.
Carb.: 46 gm. • Cholesterol: 5 mg. • Fiber: low

Peachy Fruit Salad

Dress up canned fruits or use the fresh fruit of your choice.
Can be stored for days in the refrigerator.

15-ounce can pineapple tidbits, drained

15-ounce can peaches, drained

15-ounce can pears, drained

10-ounce can mandarin oranges, drained

15-ounce can peach pie filling

1 large banana, sliced (optional)

Combine all the canned fruits in a large bowl. Stir in peach pie filling.
Store in refrigerator. When ready to serve, stir in banana slices.

99

Serves 8

Nutritional Information per serving:
Calories: 185 • Fat: 0 • Protein: 1 gm.
Carb.: 45 gm. • Cholesterol: 0 • Fiber: medium

Raspberry-Applesauce Gelatin Salad

So easy to eat and enjoy.

3-ounce package cherry gelatin
  powder
3-ounce package raspberry gelatin
  powder
2 1/2 cups boiling water

1 teaspoon lemon juice
10 ounces frozen raspberries,
  thawed
3/4 cup applesauce

In a medium saucepan, combine gelatin powders and boiling water. Stir until gelatin dissolves. Cool. Stir in lemon juice, raspberries, and applesauce. Pour mixture into mold or a bowl. Refrigerate until set.

Serves 8

Nutritional Information per serving:
Calories: 125 • Fat: 0 • Protein: 2 gm.
Carb.: 30 gm. • Cholesterol: 0 • Fiber: very low

Super Fast Pasta Salad

Colorful, easy, and flavorful.

12 ounces small pasta shells
  or rotini

16 ounces frozen broccoli,
  cauliflower, and carrot mix

2/3 cup fat-free Italian Parmesan
  salad dressing

1/4 teaspoon garlic powder

2 tablespoons minced fresh parsley

1 tablespoon minced fresh basil
  (if available)

1/4 cup black olives, sliced

freshly ground pepper to taste

1/4 cup freshly grated Parmesan
  cheese

2 tablespoons toasted pine nuts
  (optional)

101

In a large saucepan, cook pasta just until tender. Drain. Set aside. Microwave vegetables until tender-crisp. In a small bowl, mix salad dressing, garlic powder, parsley, and basil. Mix with pasta in a large bowl. Add black olives and vegetables. Cover bowl and refrigerate.

When ready to serve, top with pepper, Parmesan cheese, and toasted pine nuts (if desired).

For an extra 120 calories per serving, use regular Italian salad dressing.

Serves 6

Nutritional Information per serving:
Calories: 300 • Fat: 3 gm. • Protein: 11 gm.
Carb.: 56 gm. • Cholesterol: 5 mg. • Fiber: high

Swiss Apple Salad

Apples and cheese—sensational! A tasty light lunch.

4 medium apples

2 tablespoons lemon juice

1 cup celery, diced

8 ounces low-fat Swiss cheese,
    cut in 1/2-inch cubes

1 cup fat-free sour cream

1/8 teaspoon salt

1/8 teaspoon white pepper

1/4 teaspoon nutmeg

4 lettuce leaves

Core, quarter, and dice apples. Mix apples with lemon juice to keep from darkening. In a large bowl, combine apples, celery, cubed cheese, sour cream, salt, pepper, and nutmeg. Stir until well blended. Store in refrigerator until ready to serve. Serve on lettuce leaves.

To add an extra 175 calories per serving, use regular Swiss cheese and regular sour cream.

Serves 4

Nutritional Information per serving:
Calories: 235 • Fat: 3 gm. • Protein: 19 gm.
Carb.: 33 gm. • Cholesterol: 30 mg. • Fiber: medium

Tomato, Cheese, and Basil Salad

The combination of fresh vine-ripened tomatoes and fresh basil is one of the pleasures of summer. Serve this salad with crusty buttered bread or dip the bread in the dressing.

1 clove garlic, peeled and split in half

4 large vine-ripened tomatoes or 1 pound Roma tomatoes, cut into chunks

1 cup fresh basil leaves, rolled and cut into thin ribbon strips (chiffonade)

1/4 cup extra virgin olive oil

juice of 1 lemon

salt and freshly ground pepper to taste

1/2 pound provolone or smoked mozzarella cheese, cut into bite-sized chunks

1/4 cup toasted pine nuts (optional)

1/2 cup freshly grated Parmesan cheese

Rub the split garlic clove around the inside of a large salad bowl. Discard the garlic clove. Add tomatoes and basil. Drizzle the olive oil over tomatoes. Toss gently. Squeeze lemon juice over the mixture. Add salt and pepper. Toss gently. Cover with plastic wrap and let the mixture marinate at room temperature for about an hour.

When ready to serve, mix the cheese chunks in the salad. Place individual servings on each plate. Top with toasted pine nuts, a generous amount of Parmesan cheese, and black pepper to taste. This salad may be served with Greek or black olives and a piece of fresh fruit as a complete lunch.

Serves 4

Nutritional Information per serving:
Calories: 400 • Fat: 30 gm. • Protein: 19 gm.
Carb.: 13 gm. • Cholesterol: 60 mg. • Fiber: low

Easy Lunches

Baked Apple French Toast

Make a day ahead and serve for breakfast or lunch.

1/4 cup brown sugar
2 tablespoons butter or margarine, melted
4 slices thick-sliced bread
4 eggs
2 cups skim milk

1/4 cup sugar
1/2 teaspoon vanilla
2 large Granny Smith or cooking apples
1/4 cup sugar
1 teaspoon cinnamon

Preheat oven to 350°. Combine brown sugar and melted butter in an 8 x 8-inch baking pan. Lay bread slices flat in pan. In a mixing bowl, lightly beat eggs, milk, 1/4 cup sugar, and vanilla. Pour half of mixture over bread in pans. Peel, core, and slice apples. Arrange sliced apples on top of the bread. Pour remaining egg mixture over apples. For the topping, mix remaining 1/4 cup sugar with cinnamon. Sprinkle over top. Bake for 35 to 45 minutes or until light brown. Let stand 10 minutes before serving. Serve with maple syrup.

To add 75 extra calories per serving, add an extra 2 tablespoons of butter and substitute whole milk for the skim milk.

Serves 4

Nutritional Information per serving:
Calories: 390 • Fat: 11 gm. • Protein: 12 gm.
Carb.: 63 gm. • Cholesterol: 200 mg. • Fiber: low

Baked Egg in a Tin

Super easy and attractive way to serve eggs. Get them ready
at night, then refrigerate and pop in the oven in the morning.

4 slices bacon   salt and pepper to taste
4 eggs   dash paprika

Preheat oven to 350°. Grease 4 muffin tins or baking custard cups.
Partially fry or microwave the bacon. Arrange one bacon slice around
the inside of each tin or cup. Crack one egg into each tin or cup.
Sprinkle with salt and pepper to taste. Sprinkle with paprika. Bake for
15 to 30 minutes or until the egg is done the way you like it.

107

Serves 4

Nutritional Information per serving:
Calories: 100 • Fat: 8 gm. • Protein: 7 gm.
Carb.: 0 • Cholesterol 185 mg. • Fiber: none

Brunch Eggs

Good at any time of day.

4 slices bread, cubed
2 cups grated low-fat cheddar
   cheese
1/4 pound ham, diced, or
   1/4 pound cooked sausage

3 eggs
1 teaspoon dry mustard
1/2 teaspoon salt
1 1/2 cups skim milk
dash paprika

108

Arrange bread cubes in a buttered 8 x 8-inch baking pan. Layer on the shredded cheese and ham. Set aside. In a small bowl, beat together the eggs, dry mustard, salt, and milk. Pour over the bread mixture. Sprinkle with paprika. Refrigerate several hours or overnight. When ready to bake, preheat oven to 325°. Bake for 60 minutes or until light brown and eggs are set. Double the recipe for a 9 x 13-inch pan.

To add 100 calories per serving, use regular cheddar cheese and whole milk.

Serves 4

Nutritional Information per serving:
Calories: 350 • Fat: 11 gm. • Protein: 28 gm.
Carb.: 20 gm. • Cholesterol: 165 mg. • Fiber: very low

Chicken and Fruit Salad

Fresh fruit complements the chicken. Use your favorite
combination of fruits to prepare an easy lunch or supper salad.

4 chicken breasts without skin
1/2 cup grapes cut in half
1/2 cup pineapple chunks
1/2 cup chopped apples
1/2 cup chopped celery
1/2 cup toasted almonds, walnuts,
   or cashews

1/2 cup fat-free sour cream
1/2 cup fat-free mayonnaise
1 tablespoon lemon juice
1/4 teaspoon nutmeg
salt and pepper to taste

109

Broil or fry chicken breasts until well done. Cut chicken into cubes and
chill.

In a large bowl, combine chicken with the grapes, pineapple, apples,
celery, and nuts. In a small bowl, mix the sour cream with remaining
ingredients. Stir into chicken and fruit mixture.

Note: To cut down on preparation time, purchase fried chicken breasts
from a fried chicken fast-food restaurant. Remove skin and bones. Cut
meat into cubes. This chicken will be very moist and tasty.

To add 200 calories per serving, use regular mayonnaise and sour
cream.

Serves 4

Nutritional Information per serving:
Calories: 435 • Fat: 13 gm. • Protein: 56 gm.
Carb.: 20 gm. • Cholesterol: 135 mg. • Fiber: medium

Cornflake French Toast

A crunchy baked French toast.

3/4 cup milk

1/2 teaspoon vanilla

1/4 teaspoon salt

1 tablespoon sugar

3 eggs

1 cup cornflake crumbs

8 slices thick-sliced bread

1/4 cup butter or margarine, melted

Preheat oven to 450°. Grease a baking sheet. In a small bowl, beat together milk, vanilla, salt, sugar, and eggs. Pour mixture into a shallow bowl. Place cornflake crumbs in another shallow dish. Dip bread slices into milk mixture and then coat with cornflake crumbs. Place bread slices on greased baking sheet and drizzle with melted butter. Bake for 15 minutes or until golden brown. Turn to brown evenly, if necessary, during baking.

Serves 8

Nutritional Information per serving:
Calories: 175 • Fat: 9 gm. • Protein: 5 gm.
Carb.: 18 gm. • Cholesterol: 85 mg. • Fiber: very low

Crab-Swiss Melt

A wonderful fast lunch or tasty between-meal snack.

3/4 pound surimi seafood
  or crabmeat
1 1/2 cups grated fat-free
  processed Swiss cheese
1/2 cup fat-free mayonnaise

2 tablespoons chopped green onions
1 teaspoon lemon juice
1/4 teaspoon salt
dash Tabasco sauce
2 English muffins

Preheat oven to 375°. In a medium bowl, combine all ingredients except English muffins. Spoon mixture on English muffin halves. Place on ungreased baking pan. Bake for 10 to 15 minutes or until light brown. (May also place under the broiler until brown.) Cut each muffin into quarters or bite-sized pieces. Serve warm.

To add 275 calories per serving, use regular Swiss cheese and regular mayonnaise.

Serves 4

Nutritional Information per serving:
Calories: 230 • Fat: 1 gm. • Protein: 27 gm.
Carb.: 25 gm. • Cholesterol: 35 mg. • Fiber: very low

Creamed Tuna on Toast

Remember this one? Try other meats, fish, or poultry
in this basic sauce. Add vegetables of your choice.
Add some peas if that is the way your mother made it.

3 tablespoons butter or margarine
3 tablespoons flour
3 cups milk
1/2 teaspoon white pepper
1/2 teaspoon salt

12-ounce can water-packed white
   tuna, drained
4 hard cooked eggs, sliced
6 slices bread, toasted

Melt butter in heavy saucepan. Stir in flour and cook for at least 5 minutes. Add milk, and stir constantly until mixture comes to a boil and thickens. Reduce heat and add seasonings, tuna, and eggs. Heat through. Serve on toasted bread.

Serves 6

Nutritional Information per serving:
Calories: 315 • Fat: 14 gm. • Protein: 25 gm.
Carb.: 22 gm. • Cholesterol: 170 mg. • Fiber: very low

112

Crustless Cheesy Spinach and Bacon Pie

Great without a high-fat crust.

6 slices bacon
1/2 pound fresh mushrooms, sliced
2 cups small curd cottage cheese
1 cup shredded mozzarella cheese

4 eggs, beaten
1/2 teaspoon dried basil leaves
1/4 teaspoon garlic powder
1/4 teaspoon pepper
10 ounces frozen spinach, thawed

Preheat oven to 350°. Grease a 9-inch pie plate. In a frying pan, fry bacon until crisp. Drain and crumble. Set aside. Sauté mushrooms in the same pan. Set aside. In a large bowl, combine cottage cheese, mozzarella cheese, eggs, and seasonings. Mix well. Squeeze the thawed spinach to remove excess liquid. Add to the cheese mixture. Stir in the crumbled bacon and mushrooms. Spread into pie plate. Bake for 45 minutes or until set. Serve warm or at room temperature.

Serves 6

Nutritional Information per serving:
Calories: 230 • Fat: 14 gm. • Protein: 20 gm.
Carb.: 7 gm. • Cholesterol: 155 mg. • Fiber: low

Deviled Eggs

Keep on hand for a good protein snack.

3 eggs
3 tablespoons heavy cream
1 tablespoon sour cream
1/2 teaspoon mustard

1/4 teaspoon pepper
1/4 teaspoon salt
1 tablespoon minced chives
dash paprika

In a small saucepan, cover eggs with water, and bring to a boil. Cover and reduce heat to low. Cook for 15 minutes. Pour off water and chill quickly under cold running water. Peel hard-cooked eggs and cut in half lengthwise. Scoop out yolks and mix yolks with heavy cream, sour cream, mustard, pepper, salt, and chives. Mix well. Adjust seasoning to taste. Spoon yolk mixture back into egg whites. Sprinkle with paprika.

Serves 3

Nutritional Information per serving:
Calories: 125 • Fat: 11 gm. • Protein: 6 gm.
Carb.: 1 gm. • Cholesterol: 200 mg. • Fiber: very low

Macaroni and Cheese

Better when homemade! Try this recipe
with half cheddar and half Swiss cheese.

10 ounces uncooked elbow
macaroni
3 tablespoons butter or
margarine, divided
2 tablespoons flour
1 1/2 cups milk
8 ounces fat-free processed
American cheese
1 teaspoon grated onion (optional)

1/2 teaspoon white pepper
1/2 teaspoon dry mustard or paprika
salt and pepper to taste
1/2 cup bread crumbs
1 tablespoon finely minced
fresh parsley
2 tablespoons grated Parmesan
cheese (optional)

Preheat oven to 350°. Grease a large casserole dish. Cook macaroni in a large pot of water until barely tender. Drain. Set aside. In a heavy saucepan melt 2 tablespoons butter. Add flour and cook, stirring constantly, for at least 5 minutes. Add milk; bring to a boil and cook until mixture thickens. Stir in the shredded cheese gradually. Add onion and seasonings to taste. Mix with the cooked macaroni. Spoon into the casserole dish. For topping, combine bread crumbs with 1 tablespoon melted butter. Sprinkle bread crumbs, parsley, and Parmesan cheese on top of macaroni. Bake for 20 minutes.

For an extra 150 calories per serving, use regular cheese in place of fat-free cheese.

Serves 4

Nutritional Information per serving:
Calories: 500 • Fat: 13 gm. • Protein: 29 gm.
Carb.: 67 gm. • Cholesterol: 50 mg. • Fiber: low

Night Before French Toast

Lunch is easy when made the night before.

2 tablespoons butter or margarine
1/2 cup brown sugar
4 slices Texas-style bread
  (thickly sliced bread)

3 eggs, beaten
1 1/2 cups skim milk
1/4 teaspoon cinnamon

Grease an 8 x 8-inch baking pan. In a small saucepan, melt butter and brown sugar. Pour into baking pan. Place bread on the butter and sugar. In a small bowl, beat eggs, milk, and cinnamon together. Pour egg mixture over bread. Cover and place in refrigerator overnight. Bake uncovered at 350° for 30 minutes or until light brown. Serve with syrup and fruit.

To add 75 extra calories per serving, add an extra 2 tablespoons of butter and use whole milk.

Serves 4

Nutritional Information per serving:
Calories: 300 • Fat: 11 gm. • Protein: 10 gm.
Carb.: 42 gm. • Cholesterol: 150 mg. • Fiber: very low

116

One Dish Beef and Noodle Meal

Make a meal in one skillet.

1 pound lean ground beef
1 small onion, chopped
1/2 teaspoon salt
1/2 teaspoon pepper
30-ounce can tomatoes
2 cups frozen corn

4 ounces uncooked noodles
1 cup water
2 cups frozen peas
1 1/2 cups shredded fat-free
   cheddar cheese

In a large skillet, brown beef and chopped onions. Drain. Season with salt and pepper. Add tomatoes, corn, noodles, and water. Cover and bring to a boil. Reduce heat and simmer until noodles are done, about 10 minutes. Stir in the peas. Top with cheese. Cover and heat another 5 minutes or until cheese is melted.

To add 75 extra calories per serving, use regular cheddar cheese.

Serves 6

Nutritional Information per serving:
Calories: 410 • Fat. 17 gm. • Protein: 28 gm.
Carb.: 36 gm. • Cholesterol: 80 mg. • Fiber: high

Quesadilla—Create Your Own

Use your imagination with your leftovers. Create your own
quesadilla by adding other ingredients such as black olives, onions,
chile peppers, or tomatoes. Reduce calories by using low-fat cheese.

2 flour tortillas
cooking oil spray
1/4 cup salsa

1/3 cup Monterey Jack cheese,
  shredded
2 tablespoons fat-free sour cream

118

Lightly spray tortillas on both sides with cooking spray. Place one tortilla in small frying pan. Spread salsa and sprinkle cheese on tortilla. Top with the other tortilla. Over medium heat, fry on one side until light brown. Flip and fry on the other side until cheese is melted. Cut into wedges. Dip in sour cream and extra salsa if desired.

Serves 1

Nutritional Information per serving:
Calories: 425 • Fat: 19 gm. • Protein: 16 gm.
Carb.: 46 gm. • Cholesterol: 40 mg. • Fiber: low

Tuna Spread

3 1/2-ounce can water-packed
   tuna, drained
1 hard-cooked egg, chopped
2 tablespoons fat-free mayonnaise
1 teaspoon lemon juice
1/2 teaspoon Dijon mustard

1 tablespoon minced red onion
   (optional)
1 stalk celery, finely chopped
2 tablespoons finely chopped
   almonds (optional)
4 slices bread, toasted

Mix all ingredients and spread on toast. Serve with crisp lettuce leaves.

To add 50 calories per serving, use regular mayonnaise.

Serves 4

Nutritional Information per serving:
Calories: 145 • Fat: 5 gm. • Protein: 10 gm.
Carb.: 15 gm. • Cholesterol: 55 mg. • Fiber: low

Tuna-Noodle Casserole

A childhood memory.

3 cups uncooked noodles
1/2 cup finely chopped celery
6 1/2-ounce can water-packed
  white tuna, drained

1 can cream of mushroom soup
3/4 cup skim milk
1 cup frozen peas
2 ounces crushed potato chips

Preheat oven to 350°. Grease a large casserole dish. In a large saucepan, cook 3 cups noodles in salted boiling water until barely tender (slightly undercooked). Drain. In a large bowl, combine all ingredients except potato chips. Spoon into greased casserole dish. Top with potato chips. Bake for 30 to 40 minutes until heated thoroughly and brown on top.

For extra calories, use whole milk and more crushed potato chips.

Serves 4

Nutritional Information per serving:
Calories: 315 • Fat: 9 gm. • Protein: 21 gm.
Carb.: 38 gm. • Cholesterol: 40 mg. • Fiber: high

Main Course Meats

121

Beef Stew

So easy—no mess. One pot method.

2 pounds beef chuck roast
4 medium carrots, peeled and
   cut in large pieces
2 medium onions, cut in large pieces
2 stalks celery, cut in large pieces
3 tablespoons flour
1/2 teaspoon thyme
1 teaspoon dry mustard
1/2 teaspoon salt

1/2 teaspoon freshly ground pepper
1 bay leaf
1 cup water
1 cup beef broth
15-ounce can chopped tomatoes
1/2 cup red wine (optional)
1 cup frozen peas
1 pound fresh mushrooms, sliced

122

Preheat oven to 325°. Trim fat from meat and cut into 1- to 2-inch pieces. Combine meat with carrots, onions, and celery in a large baking dish with cover. In a small bowl, mix flour, thyme, dry mustard, salt, and pepper. Stir into meat and vegetable mixture. Add bay leaf. Stir in water, beef broth, tomatoes, and wine. Cover and bake for about 3 hours or until meat is tender. Check occasionally and add more broth if it gets too dry. Add peas and mushrooms the last 10 minutes of baking. Remove bay leaf before serving.

Serves 8

Nutritional Information per serving:
Calories: 350 • Fat: 19 gm. • Protein: 24 gm.
Carb.: 20 gm. • Cholesterol: 65 mg. • Fiber: medium

Easy One-Step Lasagna

Fast and easy to put together using uncooked lasagna noodles and commercial spaghetti sauce. Your Sicilian grandmother would probably disapprove, but who has the time?

1 pound lean ground beef
32-ounce can chopped tomatoes
2 cups canned spaghetti sauce
16 ounces uncooked lasagna
  noodles

16 ounces part skim ricotta cheese
2 cups grated mozzarella cheese
1/2 cup freshly grated Parmesan
  cheese

123

Preheat oven to 375°. Grease a 9 x 13-inch baking pan. In a large frying pan, brown ground beef. Drain. Combine drained meat with tomatoes and spaghetti sauce. Spread a thin layer of sauce on the bottom of the greased pan. Arrange half the uncooked noodles over the sauce. Spread half the ricotta cheese over the noodles. Sprinkle with half of the mozzarella cheese. Add another layer, using up the remaining noodles, sauce, ricotta cheese, and mozzarella cheese. Cover with aluminum foil. Bake covered for 50 to 60 minutes or until noodles are tender. Uncover, sprinkle with Parmesan cheese, and bake another 5 minutes. Let stand for 10 minutes before serving.

Serves 8

Nutritional Information per serving:
Calories: 640 • Fat: 29 gm. • Protein: 34 gm.
Carb.: 61 gm. • Cholesterol: 90 mg. • Fiber: medium

Ham and Sweet Potatoes

How can this be so tasty and healthy too?

8 ounces frozen or fresh small
   white onions, peeled
3 tablespoons butter or margarine
3 tablespoons flour
3 cups chicken broth
3/4 cup orange juice

1 pound lean ham, cubed
1 pound fresh sweet potatoes,
   peeled and into cut 1/2-inch cubes
1 teaspoon orange zest
salt and freshly ground pepper to
   taste

In a large frying pan, cook onions in butter until onions are translucent. Add flour and cook, stirring constantly, for 5 minutes. Add chicken broth, orange juice, ham, sweet potatoes, and orange zest. Cover the pan and simmer until potatoes are tender—about 20 to 30 minutes. Add salt and pepper to taste.

To peel small onions, place onions in boiling water for 10 to 15 seconds. Rinse under cold water. Cut off root end and pop off the peeling.

Serves 4

Nutritional Information per serving:
Calories: 430 • Fat: 16 gm. • Protein: 33 gm.
Carb.: 37 gm. • Cholesterol: 80 mg. • Fiber: medium

Ham Loaf

One of those traditional comfort recipes.

1 pound ground lean ham
1 pound ground lean pork
2 eggs, lightly beaten
1/2 cup finely minced onions
   (optional)
1/2 cup bread crumbs

1/4 cup milk
1/4 cup brown sugar
2 teaspoons Dijon mustard
1/2 teaspoon pepper
1/4 teaspoon salt

Topping

1/4 cup brown sugar
2 teaspoons Dijon mustard

125

Preheat oven to 350°. Grease a 9 x 5-inch loaf pan. In a large bowl, mix all ingredients except topping ingredients together. Spoon into the greased loaf pan. Combine topping ingredients. Spread on top of ham mixture. Bake for 1 hour or until completely done.

Serves 8

Nutritional Information per serving:
Calories: 300 • Fat: 16 gm. • Protein: 24 gm.
Carb.: 115 gm. • Cholesterol: 115 mg. • Fiber: low

Lazy Beef Stroganoff

May be called lazy, but it sure is good.

1 package (1 1/2 ounce) dry
   onion soup mix
1 can cream of mushroom soup
2 cups water

2 pounds beef stew meat
1/2 cup fat-free sour cream
1/2 pound egg noodles, cooked

Preheat oven to 325°. In a medium casserole dish, mix dry soup mix, canned soup, water, and stew meat. Cover and bake for 2 to 3 hours. Slow cooking tenderizes the meat and brings out the flavor. Check occasionally and add water if it gets too dry.

Add sour cream before serving over cooked noodles.

To add 60 calories per serving, substitute 1 cup regular sour cream for the fat-free sour cream in this recipe.

Serves 6

Nutritional Information per serving:
Calories: 540 • Fat: 27 gm. • Protein: 39 gm.
Carb.: 36 gm. • Cholesterol: 150 mg. • Fiber: low

Meat Balls with Sour Cream Sauce

A mild delicious way to serve a meat dish.

1 pound lean ground beef	1/2 cup seasoned bread crumbs
1 egg, lightly beaten	1/4 cup flour
1/4 cup milk	2 tablespoons cooking oil
1/4 teaspoon onion salt	1 can cream of mushroom soup
1/2 teaspoon salt	1/2 cup beef broth
1/2 teaspoon pepper	1/2 cup fat-free sour cream

127

In a large bowl, combine ground meat with beaten egg, milk, onion salt, salt, pepper, and seasoned bread crumbs. Roll into balls. Roll balls in flour. Heat oil in a frying pan and add meat balls. Slowly brown, turning carefully. When browned, drain off fat. Add cream of mushroom soup and beef broth. Cover and simmer on low heat until heated thoroughly. Stir in sour cream right before serving. Heat, but do not boil. Serve over egg noodles.

Serves 6

Nutritional Information per serving:
Calories: 340 • Fat: 23 gm. • Protein: 17 gm.
Carb.: 16 gm. • Cholesterol: 90 mg. • Fiber: 0

Meat Loaf—Family Favorite

A simple, tasty meat loaf recipe. For a tomato flavor,
substitute tomato sauce for the milk in this recipe.
Add seasonings of your choice.

1 1/2 pounds lean ground beef
2/3 cup bread crumbs
1/4 cup milk
2 eggs, lightly beaten

1/2 cup finely chopped onions
1 teaspoon salt
1 teaspoon pepper

Topping

1/2 cup ketchup
1 tablespoon Worcestershire sauce

1 tablespoon Dijon mustard

Preheat oven to 350°. Grease a 9 x 5-inch loaf pan. In a large mixing bowl, combine all ingredients except topping ingredients. Spoon into loaf pan. In a small bowl, mix ketchup with Worcestershire sauce and mustard. Spread sauce on top of meat. Bake for 1 hour. Pour off drippings before serving.

Serves 8

Nutritional Information per serving:
Calories: 300 • Fat: 20 gm. • Protein: 18 gm.
Carb.: 12 gm. • Cholesterol: 115 mg. • Fiber: very low

Pasta Shells
with Ham and Peas

Not fancy, but it sure tastes good.

2 cups uncooked pasta shells
1 small onion, chopped
1/2 pound fresh mushrooms, sliced
1 tablespoon butter or margarine
1 tablespoon flour
1/2 cup chicken stock
1/2 cup evaporated skim milk

1/2 pound lean ham, diced
1 cup frozen green peas
1/4 teaspoon nutmeg
salt and freshly ground pepper
  to taste
1/2 cup grated Parmesan cheese

129

In a large saucepan, cook pasta just until tender. Drain and set aside. In a medium frying pan, cook onions and mushrooms in butter until onions are translucent. Stir in flour and cook for 5 minutes. Stir in chicken stock and heat to simmering. Add the milk, ham, peas, and nutmeg. Heat until mixture is thick. Add the pasta shells and stir gently. Let the shells heat through. Adjust seasoning with salt and pepper. Top each serving with grated cheese.

For an extra 120 calories per serving, substitute heavy cream for the evaporated skim milk and add an extra 1/2 cup Parmesan cheese to the recipe.

Serves 4

Nutritional Information per serving:
Calories: 420 • Fat: 10 gm. • Protein: 28 gm.
Carb.: 54 gm. • Cholesterol: 50 mg. • Fiber: high

Pasta with Tomato and Meat Sauce

A true classic.

1 1/2 pounds lean ground beef
2 tablespoons olive oil
1 large onion, diced
1/2 red bell pepper, diced (optional)
3 cloves garlic, minced
1/2 teaspoon salt
1/2 teaspoon freshly ground pepper
1 teaspoon dried basil
1/4 teaspoon anise seed (optional)
1 bay leaf

30-ounce can chopped Italian tomatoes or Italian plum tomatoes
8-ounce can tomato sauce
1/4 cup red wine
beef broth to thin sauce (optional)
1 teaspoon sugar (optional)
salt and freshly ground pepper to taste
1 pound uncooked pasta of your choice
1/2 cup freshly grated Parmesan cheese
red pepper flakes (optional)

In a large frying pan, brown ground beef. Drain and set aside. In a heavy saucepan, heat olive oil. Cook the onions, red bell pepper, and garlic until the onions are translucent. Do not brown the garlic. Add salt, pepper, basil, anise, bay leaf, tomatoes, tomato sauce, wine, and ground beef. Heat all ingredients, then simmer on low heat for 45 minutes.

If the sauce becomes dry, add beef broth. If the sauce is too bitter, add sugar. Adjust the seasonings with salt and pepper. While the sauce is still simmering, cook the pasta in boiling salted water. Drain. Remove the bay leaf. Serve sauce over the pasta with Parmesan cheese and red pepper flakes.

Serves 6

Nutritional Information per serving (pasta with sauce):
Calories: 700 • Fat: 31 gm. • Protein: 35 gm.
Carb.: 70 gm. • Cholesterol: 90 mg. • Fiber: high

Quick Hamburger Pie

A super quick recipe.

1 pound ground beef
1 large onion, finely diced
1/2 teaspoon salt
1/2 teaspoon pepper

1 cup grated low-fat cheddar cheese
1 1/2 cups skim milk
3/4 cup reduced-fat Bisquick
3 eggs

Preheat oven to 400°. Grease a 10-inch pie pan. Brown beef and onion together in frying pan. Pour off any grease. Season with salt and pepper. Spread beef in the pie pan. Sprinkle with grated cheese. In a small bowl, beat together milk, Bisquick, and eggs. Pour over the beef and cheese. Bake for 30 minutes or until knife inserted in center comes out clean. Let stand 5 minutes before serving.

For extra calories, use your favorite regular cheese and regular Bisquick mix.

Serves 6

Nutritional Information per serving:
Calories: 380 • Fat: 25 gm. • Protein: 24 gm.
Carb.: 15 gm. • Cholesterol: 160 mg. • Fiber: very low

131

Roasted Pork Tenderloin with Maple Mustard Sauce

Pork tenderloin is as lean as chicken breast.

2 pounds pork tenderloin
1 teaspoon salt

1 teaspoon freshly ground pepper
2 tablespoons cooking oil

Sauce

1/4 cup cider vinegar
1/2 cup maple syrup
1 tablespoon Dijon mustard

1 teaspoon Worcestershire sauce
1/2 teaspoon freshly ground pepper

Preheat oven to 375°. Grease a small roasting pan. Trim fat and tough white membrane from pork tenderloins. Season with salt and pepper. In a heavy frying pan, sear tenderloin in hot oil until brown on all sides. Place tenderloin in roasting pan. Set aside. In a small saucepan, combine the sauce ingredients. Bring to a boil and cook for 5 minutes. Save half of the mixture in a small dish. Brush remaining mixture over the pork tenderloins. Bake for about 20 minutes or until meat thermometer inserted in pork registers 160°. Baste with reserved sauce. Let stand 10 minutes before serving.

Slice diagonally across grain into thin slices.

Serves 6

Nutritional Information per serving:
Calories: 270 • Fat: 7 gm. • Protein: 32 gm.
Carb.: 19 gm. • Cholesterol: 100 mg. • Fiber: 0

Shepherd's Pie

A very old recipe made easy with leftover mashed potatoes.

4 cups leftover mashed potatoes
1 egg, lightly beaten
1 pound lean ground beef
1 small onion, finely chopped
1/2 teaspoon salt
1/2 teaspoon pepper

1 tablespoon flour
1/2 cup beef broth
1 cup peeled and finely chopped
  carrots
1 cup frozen peas

Preheat oven to 350°. Grease a 10-inch pie pan. Mix mashed potatoes with beaten egg. Spread half of the potatoes in pie pan. Set aside. In a skillet, brown meat and onions. Drain. Season meat with salt and pepper. Stir flour into the meat and onions. Cook, stirring constantly, for 5 minutes. Add beef broth. Cook, stirring constantly, until it boils. Stir in carrots and peas. Pour over potatoes in the pie pan. Cover meat mixture completely with remaining mashed potatoes. Bake for 30 to 40 minutes or until light brown.

133

Serves 4

Nutritional Information per serving:
Calories: 580 • Fat: 28 gm. • Protein: 32 gm.
Carb.: 50 gm. • Cholesterol: 135 mg. • Fiber: medium

Simple Spaghetti with Meat Sauce

Super simple but tastes as good as more complex recipes.

1 1/2 pounds lean ground beef
1 large onion, finely chopped
1/2 teaspoon salt
1/2 teaspoon pepper
30-ounce can tomato sauce

1 cup water
1 tablespoon Italian seasoning
1/2 teaspoon sugar
1 pound spaghetti, cooked and
   drained

Brown meat and onions in a large heavy saucepan. Drain well. Sprinkle with salt and pepper. Add tomato sauce, water, and Italian seasoning. Bring to a boil. Reduce heat and simmer uncovered for about 1 hour or until it reaches desired thickness. Stir occasionally. Add extra water if necessary. Add sugar and adjust seasonings. Serve with cooked spaghetti.

Serves 6

Nutritional Information per serving:
Calories: 620 • Fat: 25 gm. • Protein: 31 gm.
Carb.: 68 gm. • Cholesterol: 85 mg. • Fiber: high

Poultry
and Fish

Bourbon Basted Salmon

This may be the best salmon you have ever tasted.
It browns beautifully and has a unique slightly sweet flavor.

3/4–1 pound salmon fillets or steaks

Marinade

1/4 cup brown sugar

3 tablespoons bourbon

3 tablespoons chopped onion

2 tablespoons soy sauce

2 tablespoon vegetable oil

In a small bowl, combine marinade ingredients. Pour marinade in a zipper-type plastic bag. Add salmon. Refrigerate 1 to 6 hours.

Remove salmon from marinade. In a nonstick frying pan with a small amount of cooking oil, fry salmon over low to medium heat. Fry until salmon is brown on both sides (turning once) and thoroughly done. (The salmon browns quickly because there is sugar in the marinade.)

In a small saucepan, bring marinade to a boil. Serve on the side with the salmon. This salmon is wonderful served either hot or cold.

Note: The salmon may also be grilled over charcoal, but watch carefully. It burns easily.

Serves 2

Nutritional Information per serving:
Calories: 400 • Fat: 19 gm. • Protein: 35 gm.
Carb.: 19 gm. • Cholesterol: 120 mg. • Fiber: 0

Brandy Chicken Breasts

A wonderful flavor combination for a tender, crisp chicken dish.

6 chicken breasts without skin
1/4 teaspoon garlic salt
1/4 teaspoon white pepper
1/2 pound fresh mushrooms, sliced

1 can cream of chicken soup
1 cup fat-free sour cream
1/4 cup brandy
1/2 cup grated Parmesan cheese

Preheat oven to 350°. Grease a 9 x 13-inch baking dish. Place chicken breasts in the baking dish. Sprinkle chicken with garlic salt and white pepper. Layer sliced mushrooms over chicken. Set aside. In a small bowl, combine soup, sour cream, and brandy. Pour over mushrooms. Sprinkle with Parmesan cheese. Bake for 1 hour.

For an extra 100 calories per serving, use regular sour cream and add an additional 1/2 cup of grated Parmesan cheese to the recipe.

Serves 6

Nutritional Information per serving:
Calories: 325 • Fat: 6 gm. • Protein: 57 gm.
Carb.: 10 gm. • Cholesterol: 140 mg. • Fiber: very low

Broiled Salmon with Honey-Mustard Cream Glaze

So simple but tastes so special.

1 pound salmon fillets, 1/4-inch thick
1/4 cup heavy cream

1 tablespoon honey mustard, or any type of flavored mustard
freshly ground pepper

Heat oven broiler. Grease a baking sheet. Cut salmon into 4 pieces. Place fillets on baking sheet. In a small bowl, whip the cream with a whisk until firm. Whisk in the mustard. The glaze will be the consistency of thin mayonnaise. Brush a thin layer on the salmon. Grind a small amount of black pepper onto each fillet. Broil until the cream is light brown and the salmon is thoroughly cooked (about 5 to 10 minutes).

Serves 4

Nutritional Information per serving:
Calories: 185 • Fat: 10 gm. • Protein: 23 gm.
Carb.: 1 gm. • Cholesterol: 80 mg. • Fiber: 0

Chicken and Black Bean Salad

Attractive, colorful salad with Southwestern flavor.

2 15-ounce cans black beans,
  drained
4 chicken breasts without skin,
  cooked and diced
1/2 cup diced red bell pepper
1/2 cup frozen corn

1 cup diced celery
1/2 cup finely chopped green onions
1/4 cup chopped cilantro
1/2 cup salsa
4 lettuce leaves

In a large bowl, combine drained black beans, cooked chicken, red pepper, corn, celery, onions, and cilantro. Stir in salsa. Cover and chill. Serve on a lettuce leaf.

139

Serves 6

Nutritional Information per serving:
Calories: 380 • Fat: 4 gm. • Protein: 47 gm.
Carb.: 39 gm. • Cholesterol: 85 mg. • Fiber: very high

Chicken and Dumplings

A true comfort food and family favorite.

1 whole chicken
3 stalks celery, chopped
3 large carrots, chopped
1 large onion, chopped
1 teaspoon thyme
1 teaspoon salt
1 bay leaf

3 sprigs parsley
3 cloves garlic
1 teaspoon freshly ground pepper
water to cover
1 cup frozen peas
salt and freshly ground pepper
  to taste

Dumplings

2 cups flour
3 teaspoons baking powder
1 teaspoon salt

2 eggs, beaten
2/3 cup milk

Place chicken in a large kettle. Add vegetables (except peas) and seasonings. Add enough water to cover chicken. Bring to a boil. Reduce heat. Cover and simmer for 1 to 2 hours.

Remove chicken from pot. Pour chicken broth through a strainer, pressing solids against the strainer. Remove chicken skin and bones, and pull good meat from the chicken. Return strained broth and chicken pieces back to pot. Add frozen peas. Keep the broth at a very low simmer with the lid on the kettle.

To make dumplings: Combine dry ingredients in a bowl. Stir in beaten eggs and milk. Drop rounded tablespoons of dough over hot broth and chicken, leaving room for dumplings to puff up. Cover kettle, keeping liquid at a simmer. Cook for about 15 minutes or until dumplings are light and cooked through. Adjust seasonings.

Serves 6

Nutritional Information per serving:
Calories: 550 • Fat: 26 gm. • Protein: 37 gm.
Carb.: 42 gm. • Cholesterol: 200 mg. • Fiber: low

Chicken and Wild Rice

Wild rice, chicken, apples, and raisins—
a flavorful combination in one dish.

1/2 cup wild rice
3 cups water
3 cups cubed cooked chicken
3 cups cored and diced apple,
   or 3 cups halved grapes

1/2 cup raisins
8 lettuce leaves
1 cup slivered almonds, toasted

Dressing

141

3/4 cup fat-free mayonnaise
1/2 cup orange marmalade
1/4 cup fat-free sour cream

2 tablespoons lemon juice
1/4 teaspoon nutmeg

In a heavy saucepan, combine wild rice and 3 cups of water. Bring to a boil, cover pan, and simmer for about 1 hour or until rice is tender. Drain and chill rice.

Combine chilled rice with cooked chicken, diced apples, and raisins. Cover and refrigerate. Combine all dressing ingredients in a small bowl. Refrigerate until ready to use.

When ready to serve, combine salad with dressing. Serve salad on lettuce leaves and garnish with toasted almonds.

Hint: Cooked chicken may be purchased in the frozen food section of the grocery store. Fried chicken, with the skin and bones removed, from fried chicken fast-food restaurants is a moist and flavorful alternative.

To add 140 calories per serving, use regular mayonnaise and regular sour cream in the dressing.

Serves 8

Nutritional Information per serving:
Calories: 350 • Fat: 12 gm. • Protein: 22 gm.
Carb.: 42 gm. • Cholesterol: 45 mg. • Fiber: medium

Chicken with Mushrooms in Wine Cream Sauce

No mixing—just layer chicken, mushrooms, and mild cream sauce.

2 tablespoons butter or margarine
1/2 cup finely chopped onions
  or shallots
1/2 cup white wine
1/2 cup chicken broth

1 cup half and half
4 chicken breasts, skinless and
  boneless
1/2 pound fresh mushrooms, sliced
1 teaspoon freshly ground pepper

142

Preheat oven to 325°. Grease a 9 x 9-inch baking pan. In a small frying pan, sauté onions or shallots in 1 tablespoon butter or margarine. Carefully add white wine and broth. Cook 2 minutes while stirring. (The volume of liquid will be reduced.) Add half and half. Bring to a boil, then reduce heat and cook 3 to 5 minutes, stirring until mixture thickens.

In a separate pan, brown chicken breasts in 1 tablespoon butter. Place chicken in the baking pan. Place sliced mushrooms on the chicken. Sprinkle with pepper. Spoon cream sauce over the top. Cover pan. Bake for 1 hour or until chicken is thoroughly done. Check occasionally and add more broth if it gets too dry.

Serves 4

Nutritional Information per serving:
Calories: 365 • Fat: 13 gm. • Protein: 56 gm.
Carb.: 6 gm. • Cholesterol: 160 mg. • Fiber: very low

Chicken with Orange Sauce

Fast, fruity, and refreshing way to serve chicken.

4 chicken breasts, skinless
  and boneless

1 tablespoon butter or margarine
1 cup chicken broth

Sauce

1 tablespoon cornstarch
1 teaspoon finely shredded
  orange peel
1/2 teaspoon salt
1 cup orange juice

1/4 cup chicken broth
1 tablespoon orange liqueur
  (optional)
1 teaspoon honey
2 oranges, peeled and sliced

143

Wash chicken; pat dry. In a heavy skillet, brown chicken breasts in butter or margarine. Add 1 cup chicken broth and simmer, partially covered, for about 20 minutes or until chicken is thoroughly cooked.

To prepare sauce: Mix together cornstarch, orange peel, salt, orange juice, and chicken broth in a small saucepan. Bring to a boil, stirring constantly. Reduce heat; cook until thick. Stir in orange liqueur and honey to taste. Add more broth if it gets too thick.

Add orange slices to sauce and cook until heated through. To serve, transfer chicken to serving plate. Spoon sauce over chicken, arranging orange slices on top.

Serves 4

Nutritional Information per serving:
Calories: 375 • Fat: 7 gm. • Protein: 56 gm.
Carb.: 22 gm. • Cholesterol: 140 mg. • Fiber: low

Curried Turkey Rice Salad

An interesting combination of flavors and textures.

1 cup uncooked long-grain rice
8 ounces low-fat lemon yogurt
1/2 cup fat-free mayonnaise
1 teaspoon grated lemon peel
1/4 teaspoon salt
1/4 teaspoon freshly ground pepper
1/4–1/2 teaspoon curry powder, to taste

2 cups diced white turkey meat
1/2 cup chopped toasted almonds
1/4 cup raisins
1/4 cup diced dried apricots
1/4 cup finely chopped green onions
8 ounces pineapple tidbits, drained
4 lettuce leaves

Cook rice according to package directions. Cool quickly by spreading on a cookie sheet. In a small bowl, combine yogurt, mayonnaise, lemon peel, salt, pepper, and curry powder. Set aside. In a large bowl, combine all remaining ingredients except lettuce leaves. Combine with salad dressing. Chill, then serve on lettuce leaves.

To add an extra 300 calories per serving, use regular lemon yogurt and regular mayonnaise, and add an additional 1/2 cup almonds to the recipe.

Serves 4

Nutritional Information per serving:
Calories: 540 • Fat: 12 gm. • Protein: 33 gm.
Carb.: 75 gm. • Cholesterol: 75 mg. • Fiber: low

Fried Chicken the Easy Way

The best Sunday dinner in town! This is the
easiest way to make old-fashioned fried chicken.

4 skinless chicken breasts or other
pieces (such as legs or thighs)
1 cup Bisquick baking mix

salt and freshly ground pepper to taste
1/2 teaspoon paprika
1/2 cup butter or margarine, melted

Preheat oven to 350°. Grease a 9 x 9-inch baking dish. Wash chicken
pieces. Pat dry. Roll in baking mix, and place in baking pan. Sprinkle
chicken with salt, pepper, and paprika. Pour melted butter over the
chicken. Bake for 20 minutes, then turn chicken pieces over. Bake
another 20 to 30 minutes or until chicken is brown and completely
done.

145

Serves 4

Nutritional Information per serving:
Calories: 440 • Fat: 28 gm. • Protein: 28 gm.
Carb.: 19 gm. • Cholesterol: 125 mg. • Fiber: very low

Penne with Chicken in Spicy Tomato Sauce

A wonderful combination of flavors in a one-dish meal.

1 large onion, chopped
2 cloves garlic, minced
2 tablespoons olive oil
2 chicken breasts, skinless and boneless, sliced
1 medium red pepper, sliced (optional)
14-ounce can Italian tomatoes
1/4 teaspoon dried basil
1/4 teaspoon dried oregano

1/4 teaspoon anise seed (optional)
1/4 teaspoon freshly ground pepper
salt to taste
8 ounces penne pasta (tube-shaped pasta)
1/2 cup chicken broth, if needed to thin
1/2 cup freshly grated Parmesan cheese

In a heavy saucepan, cook onions and garlic in olive oil until onions are translucent. Remove onions and garlic from pan. Put sliced chicken breast pieces in the pan. Fry until chicken is brown on all sides. Add cooked onions and garlic to pan. Add peppers, tomatoes, and seasonings. Bring to a boil, reduce heat, cover, and simmer for about 20 to 30 minutes or until chicken is thoroughly cooked. If more liquid is needed, add chicken broth or more tomatoes.

While chicken is simmering, cook the pasta. Drain. Distribute hot pasta in individual bowls. Spoon tomato-chicken mixture over pasta. Top with Parmesan cheese.

Serves 4

Nutritional Information per serving:
Calories: 440 • Fat: 9 gm. • Protein: 40 gm.
Carb.: 50 gm. • Cholesterol: 70 mg. • Fiber: medium

Quick Cashew Chicken

A favorite stir-fry.

1/4 cup soy sauce
1 1/2 teaspoons sugar
2 tablespoons cornstarch
5 green onions, diced
1 tablespoon cooking oil
3 skinless, boneless chicken breast
halves, cubed

1/2 pound fresh mushrooms, sliced
8 ounces snow peas
1 cup chicken broth
1/4 cup cashews, toasted
4 cups cooked rice

147

In a small cup, mix soy sauce, sugar, and cornstarch. Set aside. In a heavy frying pan, sauté onions in cooking oil. Add cubed chicken, and fry over high heat until light brown. Reduce heat. Add mushrooms and cook, stirring frequently, until tender. Add snow peas and chicken broth. Cook for 1 minute. Add soy sauce mixture to pan, stirring constantly until mixture thickens and is clear. Add additional broth for a thinner consistency if needed. Top with toasted cashews, and serve with rice.

To add 100 extra calories per serving, add an additional 1/2 cup of cashews to the recipe.

Serves 4

Nutritional Information per serving:
Calories: 575 • Fat: 10 gm. • Protein: 36 gm.
Carb.: 86 gm. • Cholesterol: 50 mg. • Fiber: high

Red Snapper Parmesan

1 1/2 pounds red snapper
  or orange roughy
1 egg white
1/4 cup flour
1 tablespoon minced fresh basil
  or 1 teaspoon dried basil

1/4 cup freshly grated Parmesan
  cheese
1/4 teaspoon salt
1/2 teaspoon freshly ground pepper
2 tablespoons cooking oil
1 medium lemon, quartered

Cut fish into 4 pieces. In a small bowl, lightly beat egg white. Set aside. In a shallow bowl, combine flour, basil, Parmesan cheese, salt, and pepper. Dip fish into egg whites and then coat with flour mixture. Heat cooking oil in a large nonstick skillet; add fish. Cook over medium heat for 6 to 10 minutes on each side or until light brown and fish flakes easily when tested with a fork. Serve with a lemon wedge.

Serves 4

Nutritional Information per serving:
Calories: 285 • Fat: 10 gm. • Protein: 39 gm.
Carb.: 9 gm. • Cholesterol: 65 mg. • Fiber: very low

Meatless Meals

149

Angel Hair Pasta with Garlic and Olive Oil

An easy pasta when you are not in the mood for a heavy tomato or cream sauce.

1/2 pound angel hair pasta, uncooked

3 cloves garlic, finely minced

1 tablespoon olive oil

1 cup chicken broth

1/4 teaspoon nutmeg

1 tablespoon minced fresh parsley or basil

1 teaspoon freshly ground pepper

salt to taste

3 tablespoons extra virgin olive oil

1 cup freshly grated Parmesan cheese

1/4 cup bread crumbs (optional)

red pepper flakes (optional)

1/4 cup pine nuts, toasted (optional)

In a large saucepan, heat water for pasta. In a small frying pan, cook the garlic in 1 tablespoon of olive oil, but do not brown. Add the chicken broth; bring to a boil for 1 minute, then reduce to a slow simmer. Add nutmeg, parsley, pepper, and salt. Partially cover to prevent reducing the chicken broth.

Cook pasta in boiling salted water. Drain, leaving a few tablespoons of water. Return pasta to the pan. Toss with 3 tablespoons olive oil. Add the garlic chicken broth to the pasta and toss quickly. Serve pasta in heated individual pasta bowls. Top with grated cheese, bread crumbs, a pinch of red pepper flakes, and toasted pine nuts.

Note: For a different taste, add 1 tablespoon fresh lemon juice to the chicken broth, and cut down on the salt.

Serves 4

Nutritional Information per serving without pine nuts:
Calories: 470 • Fat: 21 gm. • Protein: 20 gm.
Carb.: 50 gm. • Cholesterol: 15 mg. • Fiber: low

Broccoli Rice Casserole

Make ahead, then bake just before serving.

8 ounces shredded reduced-fat
   sharp cheddar cheese (2 cups)
2 cups cooked long-grain rice
1/2 cup finely chopped onions
1/4 cup chicken broth
1/2 teaspoon salt
1/2 teaspoon freshly ground
   pepper

1/4 teaspoon mace or nutmeg
   (optional)
20 ounces frozen chopped broccoli,
   thawed
1 large carrot, peeled and grated
1/2 cup bread crumbs
1 tablespoon margarine, melted

151

Preheat oven to 350°. Butter a 3-quart casserole dish. In a large bowl, combine all ingredients except bread crumbs and margarine. Spoon mixture into buttered casserole.

Combine bread crumbs with melted margarine. Sprinkle on top of casserole. Bake for 30 minutes.

For an extra 80 calories per serving, use regular cheese and substitute heavy cream for the skim milk.

Serves 6

Nutritional Information per serving:
Calories: 350 • Fat: 5 gm. • Protein: 14 gm.
Carb.: 8 gm. • Cholesterol: 10 mg. • Fiber: medium

Buttered Noodles

Mild flavored, high-calorie comfort noodle dish.

1/4 cup finely minced fresh parsley
1/2 teaspoon salt
1/2 teaspoon freshly ground
   pepper
dash nutmeg

8 ounces uncooked egg noodles
1/4 cup butter
2 cloves garlic, minced
1 cup freshly grated Parmesan cheese
1 cup bread crumbs, toasted

In a small bowl, combine parsley, salt, pepper, and nutmeg. Set aside. In a large saucepan, cook noodles in boiling salted water until tender. Drain. Place in a warmed bowl. While the noodles are cooking, heat the butter in a small frying pan. Add the garlic, and cook over low heat for 5 minutes. Pour the warm butter mixture over the noodles. Add the parsley mix. Toss gently. Top with cheese and bread crumbs. Serve immediately.

For an extra 150 calories per serving, add an additional 1/2 cup Parmesan cheese and an extra 1/4 cup butter to the recipe.

Serves 4

Nutritional Information per serving:
Calories: 520 • Fat: 21 gm. • Protein: 20 gm.
Carb.: 62 gm. • Cholesterol: 100 mg. • Fiber: medium

Carrot Cheddar Bake

Carrots with cheese and eggs—lots of protein and vitamins.
Choose a different vegetable if you prefer.

1 pound carrots, peeled and diced
2 cups low-fat shredded cheddar
  cheese
1/2 cup evaporated skim milk

3 eggs, beaten
1 teaspoon salt
1/4 teaspoon white pepper

Preheat oven to 350°. Butter an 8 x 8-inch casserole dish. In a saucepan, cook carrots until barely tender. Drain. Place carrots in casserole dish. Combine shredded cheese, milk, eggs, and seasonings. Pour over carrots. Bake for 45 minutes or until hot and puffy. Cut into squares to serve.

To add an extra 250 calories per serving, substitute half and half for the evaporated skim milk, use regular cheddar cheese, and add 1/4 cup melted butter to the recipe.

153

Serves 4

Nutritional Information per serving:
Calories: 210 • Fat: 7 gm. • Protein: 21 gm.
Carb.: 15 gm. • Cholesterol: 150 mg. • Fiber: medium

Chile and Cheese Frittata

A great egg meal.

1 tablespoon vegetable oil
1/2 small onion, diced
1 clove garlic, minced
5 large eggs
1/3 cup milk
1/2 teaspoon salt
dash Tabasco sauce (optional)
4 ounces whole green chiles, drained, cut into strips, seeds removed

1/2 cup canned niblet corn, drained
1/2 cup grated Monterey Jack cheese
1/2 cup grated cheddar cheese
freshly ground pepper to taste
Topping options: sour cream, salsa, sliced olives, chopped avocados, tortilla chips

154

Heat the oven broiler. In a nonstick skillet, heat oil. Add onions and garlic and cook until onions are translucent. (Do not brown the garlic.) In a medium bowl, beat eggs with milk, salt, and Tabasco sauce. Lay strips of chiles over the cooked onions in the skillet. Sprinkle corn on top. Pour the egg mixture over the onions, chiles, and corn. Keep heat low and cook until eggs are firm around the edges. Sprinkle the cheese and black pepper on the eggs. Cover the skillet, and cook about two minutes or until eggs are set in the middle (about 2 minutes). Remove the lid. Using oven mitts, hold the pan under the broiler to allow the cheese to bubble. Cut into 6 wedges. Serve with toppings of your choice.

Serves 6

Nutritional Information per serving:
Calories: 170 • Fat: 12 gm. • Protein: 10 gm.
Carb.: 5 gm. • Cholesterol: 170 mg. • Fiber: low

Easy Spinach Soufflé

A high protein, colorful soufflé. A good dish to make ahead of time.

6 eggs
2 cups cottage cheese or low-fat
  ricotta cheese
2 cups grated cheddar cheese
1/4 cup flour

1/4 cup butter or margarine, melted
1/2 teaspoon white pepper
10 ounces frozen spinach, thawed,
  squeezed dry
1/2 cup grated cheddar cheese

Preheat oven to 300°. Grease a 9 x 13-inch baking dish. In a large bowl, beat eggs. Add cottage cheese, 2 cups grated cheese, flour, melted butter, and pepper. Stir in spinach. Spoon mixture into the baking dish. Top with 1/2 cup grated cheese. Bake for 60 minutes or until set.

This can be made ahead of time and stored in the refrigerator. Bake at 325° if it has been refrigerated.

155

Serves 10

Nutritional Information per serving:
Calories: 250 • Fat: 17 gm. • Protein: 18 gm.
Carb.: 6 gm. • Cholesterol: 150 mg. • Fiber: low

Fettuccine Alfredo

Wonderful traditional taste without the fat (and healthy too!).

1/2 pound uncooked fettuccine
1/2 cup broccoli florets
1 tablespoon butter or margarine
1 small onion, finely chopped
2 cloves garlic, minced
1/2 cup sliced fresh mushrooms
1 tablespoon flour
1 1/2 cups skim milk

2 teaspoons chicken bouillon
1/2 teaspoon nutmeg
3 ounces fat-free cream cheese
1 1/2 cups freshly grated Parmesan cheese
2 tablespoons minced fresh Italian parsley
freshly ground pepper to taste

In a large saucepan, cook fettuccine in salted water until tender. Drain. In a small saucepan, blanch broccoli in salted boiling water. Drain. While fettuccine is cooking, cook onions, garlic, and mushrooms in the butter in a heavy saucepan until onions are translucent. Stir in flour and cook over low heat for 5 minutes, stirring constantly. Add milk, chicken bouillon, and nutmeg, stirring continually until mixture thickens. Add cream cheese and cooked broccoli, stirring over low heat just until mixture is hot. Pour mixture over hot cooked fettuccine. Toss lightly. Top with Parmesan cheese, parsley, and pepper to taste.

For an extra 140 calories per serving, substitute half and half for the skim milk and use regular cream cheese.

Serves 4

Nutritional Information per serving:
Calories: 450 • Fat: 13 gm. • Protein: 28 gm.
Carb.: 55 gm. • Cholesterol: 35 mg. • Fiber: medium

Fettuccine with Spinach, Mushrooms, and Garlic

Creamy fettuccine with soft vegetables, a mild taste,
and a whopping 900 calories per serving.

2 tablespoons butter or margarine
2 cloves garlic, minced
1 1/2 cups sliced fresh mushrooms
1/2 cup chicken stock
1/2 teaspoon nutmeg
10 ounces frozen spinach, thawed
  and squeezed dry

1 1/2 cups heavy cream
1 cup freshly grated Parmesan
  cheese
salt and freshly ground pepper
  to taste
1 pound fettuccine, cooked
grated Parmesan cheese for garnish

In a saucepan, melt butter, and slowly cook garlic until soft. Add mushrooms, and cook until they are no longer firm. Remove mushrooms and set aside, keeping warm. Combine chicken stock, nutmeg, and spinach in the saucepan. Stir until spinach is heated through. Cook for 5 minutes at low heat. Add the cream and Parmesan cheese. Add mushrooms back to the sauce. Stir until mixture is heated through. Thin with heated chicken stock if too thick. Add salt and pepper to taste. Pour the sauce over hot cooked fettuccine. Stir gently. Serve in individual bowls. Garnish with additional Parmesan cheese.

Serves 4

Nutritional Information per serving:
Calories: 900 • Fat: 47 gm. • Protein: 28 gm.
Carb.: 92 gm. • Cholesterol: 150 mg. • Fiber: medium

157

Italian Frittata

Great for morning, noon, or night. Choose your favorite
cheese and add vegetables and seasonings you like best.

1 yellow onion, diced
1/2 red bell pepper, diced
1/2 green bell pepper, diced
2 cloves garlic, minced
2 tablespoons olive oil
6 eggs
1/2 cup milk
1/2 teaspoon salt

1/2 teaspoon freshly ground pepper
2 tablespoons snipped fresh basil
  (if in season)
1/4 cup freshly grated Parmesan
  cheese
1 cup grated mozzarella or
  cheddar cheese
red pepper flakes (optional)

158

Turn on broiler of oven. In a heavy nonstick skillet, cook the onions,
bell peppers, and garlic in olive oil until the onions are translucent. In
a separate bowl, beat the eggs with milk. Add salt and pepper. Pour the
egg mixture over the vegetables in the hot pan. Add the basil. Cook
over medium heat for 1 minute. Reduce heat; let egg mixture cook until
the edges are set. Lift the edges and let any egg mixture run under the
omelet. Sprinkle with cheeses and red pepper flakes if desired. Finish
the omelet in the oven by holding the pan close to the broiler heat. (Be
sure you wear oven mitts.) Can be served warm or at room temperature.

For an extra 100 calories per serving, add an extra 1 cup cheddar
cheese to the recipe.

Serves 4

Nutritional Information per serving:
Calories: 300 • Fat: 23 gm. • Protein: 18 gm.
Carb.: 6 gm. • Cholesterol: 300 mg. • Fiber: very low

Linguine with Fresh Tomato and Basil Sauce

4 cloves garlic, minced
2 tablespoons olive oil
8 large fresh tomatoes, peeled, chopped, and seeded
1/4 cup red wine
1/2 cup chicken broth
1/4 cup fresh basil leaves

salt and freshly ground pepper to taste
1 pound linguine, uncooked
1 cup freshly grated Parmesan cheese
freshly ground pepper
red pepper flakes (optional)

Cook garlic slowly in olive oil in a medium skillet. Do not brown. Add tomatoes, wine, broth, and seasonings. Bring sauce to a boil, then quickly reduce heat; cover and simmer for 15 to 20 minutes. When ready to serve, cook pasta in boiling salted water just until tender. Drain, leaving 2 tablespoons cooking water. Toss pasta with tomato sauce. Serve immediately in heated bowls or plates. Top each serving with Parmesan cheese, pepper, and red pepper flakes.

Note: To peel fresh tomatoes, make a small cross slit at the bottom of the tomato. Plunge in boiling water for 5 seconds to loosen skin.

For an extra 110 calories, add an extra 1/4 cup olive oil and another 1/2 cup Parmesan cheese to the recipe.

Serves 6

Nutritional Information per serving:
Calories: 425 • Fat: 10 gm. • Protein: 18 gm.
Carb.: 65 gm. • Cholesterol: 10 mg. • Fiber: medium

Meatless Chili

This chili is a wonderful tasty alternative to regular chili.

2 tablespoons cooking oil
2 medium onions, chopped
1/2 medium green pepper, chopped
1 medium red pepper, chopped
2 stalks celery, chopped
3 cloves garlic, minced
30-ounce can stewed tomatoes
1/2 teaspoon oregano flakes
1 teaspoon cumin
1 tablespoon chili powder

1 teaspoon freshly ground black pepper
16-ounce can kidney beans, drained
16-ounce can cannellini beans, drained
16-ounce can black beans, drained
2 fresh jalapeño chiles, seeds removed, minced (optional)
10 ounces frozen corn (optional)
salt to taste

Heat oil in a large saucepan. Add onions, peppers, celery, and garlic. Cook until tender. Add tomatoes, oregano, cumin, chili powder, and black pepper. Simmer for 15 minutes. Add beans and jalapeño chiles; simmer for 15 minutes. If using, add corn and cook for 5 to 10 minutes. Add salt to taste.

Topping ideas: Serve with fresh cilantro, sour cream, fresh chopped tomatoes, minced jalapeño chiles, or shredded cheese.

For an extra 60 calories per serving, add 1/2 cup shredded cheese and 1/4 cup sour cream on top of each serving.

Serves 8

Nutritional Information per serving:
Calories: 430 • Fat: 4 gm. • Protein: 24 gm.
Carb.: 74 gm. • Cholesterol: 0 • Fiber: very high

Meatless Pasta Sauce

A light tomato sauce with vegetables. Serve with pasta of your choice.

4 tablespoons olive oil
1 large onion, diced
1/2 medium green pepper, diced
1 medium red pepper, diced
3 cloves garlic, minced
30-ounce can Italian tomatoes
1/4 cup red wine
1/4 cup chicken stock
1 bay leaf

1/4 cup fresh basil or 2 teaspoons
  dried basil
1/2 teaspoon anise seed (optional)
freshly ground pepper to taste
salt and sugar to taste
crushed red pepper flakes (optional)
1/2 cup sliced black olives (optional)
grated Parmesan or Romano cheese

161

In a large saucepan, heat olive oil. Add the onions and peppers. Sauté for 1 minute, then reduce heat and cook until onions are translucent. Add garlic and cook for an additional 3 minutes, stirring constantly. Do not brown the garlic. Add tomatoes, wine, stock, bay leaf, basil (if using fresh basil wait until the last 10 minutes of cooking), anise, and black pepper. Simmer for 20 minutes. Taste the sauce; add salt to taste. If it tastes too bitter, add 1 teaspoon sugar. Cook additional 10 minutes.

For a spicy flavor, add a pinch of crushed red pepper flakes. Black olives can be added to the sauce in the last few minutes of cooking if desired. Remove bay leaf. Serve sauce with penne, rigatoni, or ziti pasta. Top with grated Parmesan or Romano cheese.

Serves 4

Nutritional Information per serving:
Calories: 320 • Fat: 19 gm. • Protein: 5 gm.
Carb.: 32 gm. • Cholesterol: 0 • Fiber: high

Pasta and Vegetables

Pasta in a light olive oil and chicken broth
with a hint of nutmeg and basil.

1 pound frozen mixed vegetables,
  any variety
12 ounces uncooked pasta such
  as rotini, bowtie, or fusilli
1 cup chicken stock
1 tablespoon lemon juice
1 teaspoon dried basil
1/2 teaspoon freshly ground
  pepper
1/4 teaspoon nutmeg

1/2 teaspoon garlic powder
2 tablespoons finely minced parsley
salt and freshly ground pepper
  to taste
3 tablespoons extra virgin olive oil
1/4 cup bread crumbs, toasted
1/2 cup freshly grated Parmesan
  cheese
red pepper flakes (optional)

162

Cook the vegetables in the microwave until crisp tender—do not over-cook. Set aside. Cook pasta in rapidly boiling salted water. In another pan, while the pasta is cooking, heat stock, lemon juice, basil, pepper, nutmeg, and garlic powder for 5 minutes. Add the vegetables and pars-ley. Simmer for 2 to 3 minutes. Adjust the seasonings with additional pepper and salt. Keep warm. When the pasta is cooked, drain, leaving 2 tablespoons of the water. Add back to the pot. Toss with olive oil. Pour vegetable mix over the pasta and stir gently. Place each serving in a warmed pasta bowl. Top with bread crumbs and a generous serving of freshly grated Parmesan cheese. Add a pinch of red pepper flakes for extra zest.

Note: Frozen vegetable mixes such as broccoli, cauliflower, and carrots or other mixed varieties all work well with these seasonings.

For an extra 50 calories per serving, add an extra 1/2 cup Parmesan cheese to the recipe.

Serves 4

Nutritional Information per serving:
Calories: 570 • Fat: 16 gm. • Protein: 21 gm.
Carb.: 86 gm. • Cholesterol: 10 mg. • Fiber: high

Pepper Quiche

9-inch pie crust, unbaked
1 medium onion, finely chopped
1/2 medium green pepper, diced
1/2 medium red pepper, diced
1 tablespoon butter or margarine
1 cup grated low-fat Swiss cheese

1/4 cup minced fresh parsley
3 eggs
1 1/4 cups milk
1/2 teaspoon salt
1/2 teaspoon white pepper
1/2 teaspoon nutmeg

Preheat oven to 400°. Prick bottom of unbaked pie shell and bake for 5 minutes. Set aside. In a frying pan, sauté onions and peppers in butter until onions are translucent. Spoon into partially baked pie shell. Sprinkle with grated cheese and parsley. In a medium bowl, beat eggs; stir in milk and seasonings. Pour over vegetables and cheese in the pie shell. Bake at 375° for 40 minutes or until set and light brown.

To add 75 calories per serving, substitute half and half for the milk and use regular Swiss cheese in place of the low-fat cheese.

163

Serves 6

Nutritional Information per serving:
Calories: 255 • Fat: 15 gm. • Protein: 12 gm.
Carb.: 18 gm. • Cholesterol: 110 mg. • Fiber: very low

Red Beans and Rice

1 large onion, diced
4 stalks celery, sliced
2 cloves garlic, minced
1 medium green pepper, diced
2 tablespoons olive oil
15-ounce can chopped tomatoes
1/2 cup chicken stock
1 tablespoon chili powder
1 teaspoon freshly ground black
  pepper

1/2 teaspoon oregano
1 bay leaf
15-ounce can kidney beans,
  drained
salt to taste
Tabasco sauce to taste
4 cups cooked rice

In a large frying pan, using low heat, cook onions, celery, garlic, and green pepper in olive oil until onions are translucent. Add tomatoes, chicken stock, chili powder, pepper, oregano, bay leaf, and kidney beans. Bring to a boil, then reduce heat and simmer for 20 minutes. Remove bay leaf. Adjust seasoning with salt and Tabasco sauce. Serve over cooked rice or mix bean mixture with rice before serving.

For an extra 200 calories per serving, top each serving with 1/2 cup grated cheddar cheese.

Serves 6

Nutritional Information per serving:
Calories: 575 • Fat: 6 gm. • Protein: 15 gm.
Carb.: 115 gm. • Cholesterol: 0 • Fiber: high

Rice Pilaf

Toasted rice and walnuts with a hint of garlic.

1/2 cup chopped almonds
1/2 cup diced onions
1 clove garlic, minced
4 tablespoons olive oil
1 cup uncooked rice

2 cups chicken broth, heated
1/2 cup golden raisins (optional)
1/2 teaspoon salt
1/2 teaspoon freshly ground
    black pepper

Toast almonds in the oven at 300° for about 10 minutes or until light brown. Watch carefully. Set aside. In a medium saucepan, cook onions and garlic in olive oil until tender. Add the rice and cook for about 3 minutes or until lightly toasted, stirring constantly to prevent rice from sticking or burning. Carefully add hot chicken broth; add salt and pepper. Bring to a boil, reduce heat, and cover. Simmer until rice is tender and has absorbed all the liquid, about 15 to 20 minutes. Stir in the toasted almonds and raisins.

For an extra 150 calories per serving, add an extra 1/2 cup of almonds and 1/4 cup melted butter or margarine to the cooked rice.

Serves 4

Nutritional Information per serving:
Calories: 425 • Fat: 18 gm. • Protein: 11 gm.
Carb.: 55 gm. • Cholesterol: 0 • Fiber: low

Spinach Cheese Pie

Spinach made elegant.

10 ounces frozen spinach
3 ounces cream cheese, softened
1 cup milk
1/2 cup soft bread crumbs
1/4 cup grated Parmesan cheese
2 eggs, lightly beaten
2 tablespoons butter or margarine
1 large onion, finely chopped

1/2 pound mushrooms, finely chopped
1/4 teaspoon nutmeg
1 teaspoon salt
1/2 teaspoon white pepper
1/2 cup grated low-fat Swiss cheese
9-inch pie crust, unbaked

Preheat oven to 400°. Thaw spinach and squeeze dry. In a bowl, blend cream cheese with milk. Add bread crumbs, Parmesan cheese, and eggs. Stir in the spinach. Set aside. In a frying pan, cook onions and mushrooms in butter until onions are translucent. Stir in nutmeg, salt, and pepper. Add onion mixture to the spinach mixture. Spoon into unbaked pie shell. Top with Swiss cheese. Bake for 10 minutes, then turn oven down to 350° and bake another 30 minutes or until pie is set and slightly brown.

For an extra 60 calories per serving, add an extra 1 cup grated Parmesan cheese to the recipe.

Serves 6

Nutritional Information per serving:
Calories: 390 • Fat: 22 gm. • Protein: 15 gm.
Carb.: 33 gm. • Cholesterol: 100 mg. • Fiber: medium

Sweet and Sour Tofu

Tofu will look and taste like chicken in this dish. You won't miss
the chicken or pork when you combine golden brown tofu cubes
with other traditional sweet and sour ingredients.

10 ounces firm tofu
1 teaspoon cornstarch
2 tablespoons vegetable oil
1 cup pineapple juice
2/3 cup cider vinegar
1/3 cup soy sauce
2/3 cup brown sugar

1/2 teaspoon salt
2 tablespoons cornstarch
2 medium green peppers, diced
8 ounces pineapple chunks in juice
1 cup cherry tomatoes
4 cups cooked rice

167

Cut tofu into small bite-sized cubes. Toss with 1 teaspoon cornstarch.
In a nonstick frying pan, sauté tofu in the oil until golden brown. Set
aside. Combine pineapple juice, vinegar, soy sauce, brown sugar, salt,
and 2 tablespoons cornstarch in a heavy saucepan, stirring until mixture
is blended. Bring to a boil, stirring constantly. Cook until mixture thickens and is clear. Add green pepper and pineapple chunks. Simmer 5
minutes. Add cherry tomatoes and hot tofu. Stir gently and heat about
1 minute. Serve over rice.

Serves 4

Nutritional Information per serving:
Calories: 600 • Fat: 10 gm. • Protein: 18 gm.
Carb.: 110 gm. • Cholesterol: 0 • Fiber: medium

Vegetable Melt

A great way to serve fresh vegetables. Choose
any vegetables and top with your favorite cheese.

8 small red potatoes
20 baby carrots
1 cup cauliflower florets
1 cup broccoli florets
8 asparagus spears

2 cups shredded low-fat Swiss
  cheese
1/8 teaspoon paprika
salt and freshly ground pepper
  to taste

Preheat oven to 350°. Cook all vegetables until tender-crisp. Arrange attractively in shallow baking dish or individual baking dishes. Top with shredded cheese. Sprinkle with paprika, salt, and pepper. Bake for 15 minutes or until heated through.

To increase calories by 100 calories per serving, use regular cheese.

Serves 4

Nutritional Information per serving:
Calories: 275 • Fat: 3 gm. • Protein: 22 gm.
Carb.: 40 gm. • Cholesterol: 20 mg. • Fiber: high

Vegetable Quiche in Rice Crust

A low-calorie quiche with a crunchy rice crust.

2 cups cooked rice
1 egg, beaten
1/2 cup shredded low-fat Swiss
    cheese
1 cup chopped broccoli
1 cup chopped cauliflower
1/2 cup shredded carrots

1 cup shredded low-fat Swiss
    cheese
2 eggs
1 cup milk
1/4 teaspoon nutmeg
1/2 teaspoon salt
1/2 teaspoon pepper

169

Preheat oven to 350°. Grease a 9-inch pie pan. In a medium bowl, combine cooked rice, 1 beaten egg, and 1/2 cup cheese. Press into greased pie pan. Bake for 5 minutes. In a saucepan, cook broccoli and cauliflower in boiling water for 3 minutes. Drain well. Spoon into crust. Layer with carrots and 1 cup cheese. In a small bowl, beat 2 eggs, milk, and seasonings together. Pour over vegetables and cheese. Bake for 40 minutes or until light brown and eggs are set. Let stand 5 minutes before serving.

To add 65 calories per serving, use regular Swiss cheese.

Serves 6

Nutritional Information per serving:
Calories: 200 • Fat: 5 gm. • Protein: 14 gm.
Carb.: 25 gm. • Cholesterol: 105 mg. • Fiber: low

Wild Rice with Apples, Apricots, and Pecans

A great combination of flavors and textures.

2 cups uncooked wild rice
2 quarts water
1 large apple, chopped
1/2 cup chopped dried apricots
1 cup chopped pecans

1 teaspoon ground ginger
1 teaspoon ground nutmeg
1 teaspoon salt
1/4 cup butter or margarine,
    melted

170

Preheat oven to 350°. Butter a 3-quart casserole dish. In a large saucepan, combine wild rice and water. Bring to a boil, then reduce heat and simmer for 45 minutes or until rice is tender. Drain. Set aside. In a large bowl, combine all ingredients. Spoon into the casserole dish. Bake for 30 minutes.

Serves 8

Nutritional Information per serving:
Calories: 275 • Fat: 11 gm. • Protein: 7 gm.
Carb.: 40 gm. • Cholesterol: 15 mg. • Fiber: high

Vegetables

Baked Stuffed Potatoes

Wonderful homemade flavor even if made ahead and frozen.

4 large baking potatoes
1/2 cup milk
1 cup shredded cheddar cheese,
  divided

1/2 teaspoon white pepper
salt to taste
dash paprika
2 tablespoons finely chopped chives

Preheat oven to 425°. Wash potatoes and prick with a fork. Bake for about 1 hour or until fork-tender in the middle of the potato and skin is crisp. Cut potatoes in half. Scoop potato pulp into a large bowl, leaving shell intact. Beat the hot potatoes with milk, using an electric mixer. Add additional milk if necessary to make a light, fluffy mashed potato. Add 1/2 cup shredded cheese, white pepper, and salt. Spoon mixture back into 6 of the potato shells; discard remaining shells. Sprinkle remaining shredded cheese on top. Sprinkle with paprika and chives.

When ready to serve, reheat in oven for about 20 minutes or until hot.

Reheat thawed frozen potatoes at 350° for 30 minutes before serving. They will taste like you just made them.

For an extra 70 calories per serving, add 1/4 cup of butter or margarine when whipping the potatoes.

172

Serves 6

Nutritional Information per serving:
Calories: 150 • Fat: 7 gm. • Protein: 7 gm.
Carb.: 15 gm. • Cholesterol: 25 mg. • Fiber: low

Beets à l'Orange

Beets and oranges are a wonderful flavor combination.

1/2 cup orange juice
2 tablespoons lemon juice
1 tablespoon vinegar
1/2 teaspoon salt
1/4 teaspoon pepper
1 tablespoon sugar

1 tablespoon cornstarch
1 tablespoon water
16-ounce can small whole beets,
    drained
2 tablespoons butter or margarine

In a heavy saucepan, combine orange juice, lemon juice, vinegar, salt, pepper, and sugar. Set aside. In a small bowl, mix cornstarch and water to a smooth paste. Stir into juice mixture. Cook mixture over medium heat, stirring constantly, until thick and clear. Add drained beets and butter. Heat thoroughly.

173

Serves 4

Nutritional Information per serving:
Calories: 125 • Fat: 6 gm. • Protein: 1 gm.
Carb.: 17 gm. • Cholesterol: 15 mg. • Fiber: low

Cauliflower, Italian Style

An unusual side dish. Cauliflower is a bland vegetable and can be made more flavorful with garlic, nutmeg, and Parmesan cheese.

1 large cauliflower head, remove core and dark green leaves

3 tablespoons olive oil, divided

2 cloves garlic, minced

1/2 cup chicken stock

1/4 teaspoon nutmeg

freshly ground pepper and salt to taste

1/2 cup freshly grated Parmesan cheese

1/2 cup bread crumbs, toasted

pinch red pepper flakes (optional)

174

Separate cauliflower into florets. Soak in cold water for 10 minutes. Cook florets in a large pot of boiling salted water until tender (5 to 7 minutes). Drain thoroughly. Toss with 2 tablespoons olive oil. In a small saucepan, cook garlic in 1 tablespoon olive oil on low heat until garlic is soft. Add chicken stock, nutmeg, and black pepper. Bring to a boil, then reduce heat and simmer for 3 minutes. Pour mixture over cauliflower and season with salt. Place the mixture in a warmed serving bowl. Top with Parmesan cheese and bread crumbs. Sprinkle with red pepper flakes for a spicy zip.

Note: For more calories, break the cauliflower into smaller pieces. After mixing with the olive oil and stock, add 2 cups cooked tiny pasta shells. Add additional 1/2 cup heated chicken stock to make a soupier mixture. Top each serving with bread crumbs, nutmeg, black pepper, and Parmesan cheese.

Serves 4

Nutritional Information per serving:
Calories: 200 • Fat: 14 gm. • Protein: 7 gm.
Carb.: 11 gm. • Cholesterol: 10 mg. • Fiber: very low

Corn Pudding

An easy southern corn pudding recipe.

3 tablespoons butter or margarine   3 eggs
2 tablespoons sugar   1 3/4 cups milk
2 tablespoons flour   4 cups frozen corn
1 teaspoon salt

Preheat oven to 325°. Butter an 8-inch square baking pan. Blend butter, sugar, flour, and salt. In a separate bowl, beat eggs. Add milk. Stir in the corn. Add the flour mixture to the corn mixture, stirring well. Pour into baking pan. Place the baking pan in a pan of water in the oven. Bake for 45 minutes or until firm.

For an extra 120 calories per serving, substitute half and half for the milk and add an extra 2 tablespoons of butter or margarine to the recipe.

Serves 6

Nutritional Information per serving:
Calories: 260 • Fat: 11 gm. • Protein: 8 gm.
Carb.: 32 gm. • Cholesterol: 175 mg. • Fiber low

175

Do-Ahead Mashed Potatoes

These potatoes are wonderful. Even when made days ahead of time, they taste like you just made them. Good to keep on hand in the refrigerator for a quick warming whenever you are in the mood for great mashed potatoes.

5 large russet potatoes, peeled
  and quartered
1/3 cup skim milk
1/2 cup fat-free sour cream

3 ounces fat-free cream cheese
1/4 teaspoon white pepper
salt to taste

Butter a casserole dish. Boil potatoes in large saucepan until tender. Drain. In a large bowl, mash potatoes using an electric mixer. Mix in milk and beat until fluffy. Beat in remaining ingredients. Add extra milk if needed for a smooth, light consistency. Transfer potatoes to the casserole dish. Cover and refrigerate.

On the day of serving, heat potatoes in 350° oven until hot—about 30 minutes. They can also be reheated in a microwave.

For an extra 140 calories per serving, use regular sour cream and regular cream cheese in this recipe.

Serves 5

Nutritional Information per serving:
Calories: 110 • Fat: 0 • Protein: 6 gm.
Carb.: 21 gm. • Cholesterol: 5 mg. • Fiber: low

Island Yams

Sweet nutrition.

3 large yams or sweet potatoes, peeled and quartered

1/4 cup butter or margarine

9 ounces crushed pineapple, drained

1 teaspoon orange rind

2 tablespoons orange juice

1/2 teaspoon cinnamon

1/4 teaspoon ginger or cloves

3/4 teaspoon salt

2 tablespoons brown sugar

1/4 cup flaked coconut

Preheat oven to 350°. Grease a 2-quart baking dish. In a large saucepan, cook potatoes in boiling water until fork-tender. Drain. In a large bowl, mash potatoes, and stir in butter, pineapple, orange rind, orange juice, cinnamon, ginger, and salt. Spoon into the baking dish. Sprinkle with brown sugar and coconut. Cover and bake covered for 30 minutes.

177

Serves 6

Nutritional Information per serving:
Calories: 160 • Fat: 8 gm. • Protein: 1 gm.
Carb.: 22 gm. • Cholesterol: 20 mg. • Fiber: low

Italian Seasoned Canned Potatoes

Makes even canned potatoes taste wonderful,
but you can also use boiled fresh potatoes.

16-ounce can whole potatoes,
  drained
1/4 cup butter or margarine,
  melted
1/4 teaspoon pepper

1/2 teaspoon Italian seasoning
1/4 teaspoon garlic salt
1/4 cup chopped fresh parsley
dash cayenne pepper (optional)

Preheat oven to 375°. Butter a small casserole or baking pan. Drain the canned potatoes and spoon into the casserole bowl. Set aside. In a small cup, combine melted butter with all of the seasonings. Pour over potatoes and toss until coated. Bake for 20 to 25 minutes or until light brown. Stir potatoes after 10 minutes. May also brown briefly under the broiler.

For an extra 130 calories per serving, add an additional 1/4 cup margarine to the recipe.

Serves 3

Nutritional Information per serving:
Calories: 230 • Fat: 15 gm. • Protein: 3 gm.
Carb.: 21 gm. • Cholesterol: 41 mg. • Fiber: low

Maple Pecan
Sweet Potato Casserole

2 pounds sweet potatoes, peeled
  and quartered
1/4 cup maple syrup
2 tablespoons butter or margarine

1/2 cup 2% milk
1/2 teaspoon salt
1/4 teaspoon nutmeg
1/2 teaspoon cinnamon

Topping (optional)

1/4 cup brown sugar
2 tablespoons flour

1 tablespoon margarine
1/4 cup chopped pecans

Preheat oven to 350°. Butter a 2-quart casserole dish. In a large saucepan, cook potatoes in water until fork tender. In a large mixing bowl, combine sweet potatoes with maple syrup, butter, milk, salt, nutmeg, and cinnamon. Beat with an electric mixer.

Transfer to the casserole dish. For the topping, combine the sugar and flour in a bowl. Cut in the margarine. Stir in pecans. Sprinkle topping on potatoes. Bake for 30 minutes. This can be made several days ahead of time and stored in the refrigerator.

Note: Canned, drained sweet potatoes can be substituted for boiled fresh potatoes.

For an extra 100 calories per serving, substitute half and half for the 2% milk, and add an additional 1/4 cup margarine and an extra 1/4 cup pecans to the recipe.

Serves 6

Nutritional Information per serving:
Calories: 260 • Fat: 8 gm. • Protein: 3 gm.
Carb.: 44 gm. • Cholesterol: 10 mg. • Fiber: medium

Marinated Vegetables

A variety of vegetables can be used. Choose your
favorite to keep on hand. Keeps well for a week.

1 head cauliflower
1 bunch broccoli
1 pound fresh mushrooms

10-ounce can black olives, drained
2 cups cherry tomatoes
1 large cucumber, sliced

Marinade

1 cup white wine vinegar
1 cup olive oil
1 teaspoon garlic salt
1 teaspoon white pepper

1 tablespoon sugar
1 tablespoon dill weed
1 teaspoon salt

Wash cauliflower and broccoli. Cut into bite-size florets, discarding
tough stems. In a large saucepan, blanch cauliflower and broccoli florets in salted boiling water for 3 to 5 minutes. Plunge into cold water to
chill quickly. Drain well. Wash and dry mushrooms. Cut mushrooms in
half. Combine mushrooms, cauliflower, and broccoli with black olives
and cherry tomatoes in a large zipper-type plastic bag. In a large jar, mix
all marinade ingredients together. Pour marinade into bag with vegetables. Refrigerate for 12 hours before serving.

Add cucumber just before serving.

Serves 12

Nutritional Information per serving:
Calories: 220 • Fat: 20 gm. • Protein: 2 gm.
Carb.: 8 gm. • Cholesterol: 0 • Fiber: high

Minted Peas

Peas and mint—a perfect flavor combination for spring.

10 ounces frozen baby peas
1 tablespoon butter or margarine
1/4 cup chicken stock

salt and pepper to taste
2 tablespoons snipped fresh
mint leaves

In a medium saucepan, place peas, butter, chicken stock, salt, and pepper. Heat gently to a slow simmer. Add the mint. Cover and cook for 2 to 3 minutes or until the peas are just done. Adjust seasoning with salt and pepper. Mixture can be pureed in a food processor or blender if necessary.

For an extra 50 calories per serving, add an extra 2 tablespoons of butter to the recipe.

Serves 4

Nutritional Information per serving:
Calories: 80 • Fat: 3 gm. • Protein: 4 gm.
Carb.: 10 gm. • Cholesterol: 10 mg. • Fiber: medium

181

Orange Brandy Carrots

A sweet delight!

36 baby carrots
2 tablespoons Grand Marnier
   orange liqueur
1/4 cup brandy

1/4 cup honey
2 tablespoons lemon juice
2 tablespoons minced parsley

Butter a small casserole dish. In a large saucepan, cook carrots just until crisp-tender in a small amount of salted water. Drain. Place carrots in casserole dish. Combine liqueur, brandy, honey, and lemon juice in small saucepan. Bring to boil and continue to boil gently until mixture is reduced by a third. Pour over carrots. Cover dish, and marinate in the refrigerator overnight. Reheat in 350° oven for 20 minutes or microwave until hot. Sprinkle with parsley.

Serves 3

Nutritional Information per serving:
Calories: 165 • Fat: 0 • Protein: 2 gm.
Carb.: 39 gm. • Cholesterol: 0 • Fiber: low

Potato Casserole

The best potatoes ever!

2 pounds frozen hashed brown
  potatoes
1 small onion, finely chopped
1 teaspoon salt
1 teaspoon pepper
10-ounce can cream of chicken soup

1 cup fat-free sour cream
8 ounces low-fat cheddar cheese,
  grated
1 1/2 cups cornflake crumbs
1/4 cup butter or margarine, melted

Preheat oven to 300°. Grease a 9 x 13-inch baking pan. In a large bowl, gently stir together the potatoes, onions, salt, pepper, soup, and sour cream. Spoon into baking pan. Sprinkle with cheddar cheese. Sprinkle cornflakes on top of cheese. Drizzle with melted butter. Bake at 300° for 1 1/4 hours or at 350° for 1 hour.

183

For an extra 50 calories per serving, use regular sour cream and regular cheddar cheese.

Serves 12

Nutritional Information per serving:
Calories: 270 • Fat: 15 gm. • Protein: 8 gm.
Carb.: 25 gm. • Cholesterol: 40 mg. • Fiber: very low

Scalloped Potatoes

Slimmed down version of scalloped potatoes.

4 large baking potatoes, peeled
1/2 cup grated Parmesan cheese
1/2 teaspoon freshly ground pepper
1/4 teaspoon nutmeg

1 teaspoon salt
2 cups milk, divided
1/2 cup nonfat sour cream

Preheat oven to 350°. Grease a 9 x 9-inch baking pan. Thinly slice potatoes. In a small bowl, mix together Parmesan cheese, pepper, nutmeg, and salt. In the baking pan, layer a third of the potatoes and top with a third of the cheese mixture. Pour 1 cup of milk over potatoes and cheese. Repeat. Add the last third of potatoes. Top with the last third of the cheese mixture. Spread the sour cream on the potatoes. Cover with foil. Bake for 1 hour. Turn oven up to 375°. Remove the foil and bake an additional 15 minutes to brown the potatoes.

For an extra 130 calories per serving, substitute half and half for the milk and use regular sour cream.

Serves 4

Nutritional Information per serving:
Calories: 220 • Fat: 5 gm. • Protein: 12 gm.
Carb.: 32 gm. • Cholesterol: 20 mg. • Fiber: low

Spicy Oven Roasted Potatoes

Add spice to the life of ordinary baked potatoes.

vegetable oil cooking spray
4 large baking potatoes
2 tablespoons olive oil
1/2 teaspoon sugar
1/4 teaspoon garlic powder

1/2 teaspoon dried rosemary
1/2 teaspoon freshly ground
 pepper
1 teaspoon salt

Preheat oven to 375°. Spray a baking pan with cooking spray. Wash and cube potatoes. Place potato cubes in large bowl. Drizzle potatoes with oil. Add all remaining ingredients. Stir to coat. Arrange potatoes in one layer on the baking pan. Bake for 20 minutes, then turn potatoes. Bake an additional 15 to 20 minutes or until light brown.

185

Serves 4

Nutritional Information per serving:
Calories: 160 • Fat: 7 gm. • Protein: 3 gm.
Carb.: 23 gm. • Cholesterol: 0 • Fiber: low

Squash and Pumpkin Timbales

Now this is a great way to serve up some vitamin A.

1 cup canned pumpkin
1 cup butternut squash,
   cooked and mashed
5 eggs, beaten
1 cup evaporated skim milk
1/2 cup chicken broth
1/2 teaspoon salt

1/2 teaspoon paprika
1/4 teaspoon nutmeg
1/4 teaspoon cinnamon or cloves
1/4 teaspoon freshly ground
   pepper
1/4 cup toasted pumpkin seeds
   or sunflower seeds (optional)

Preheat oven to 325°. Grease 6 individual custard baking cups (ramekins). In a large bowl, combine pumpkin, mashed squash, beaten eggs, milk, broth, salt, paprika, nutmeg, cinnamon, and pepper. Stir to blend. Divide mixture evenly among the custard cups. Place custard cups in a baking pan. Set the pan on oven rack and pour enough hot water into pan to reach halfway up sides of custard dishes. Bake for 40 minutes or until a knife inserted into the center comes out clean. Be careful of the steam produced when opening the oven door.

To serve, invert cups onto plates. Garnish with additional nutmeg and toasted seeds.

For an extra 100 calories per serving, substitute heavy cream for the evaporated skim milk.

Serves 6

Nutritional Information per serving without the seeds:
Calories: 130 • Fat: 4 gm. • Protein: 10 gm.
Carb.: 15 gm. • Cholesterol: 150 mg. • Fiber: low

Sweet Potato Wedges

Serve this vitamin A rich vegetable with sour cream for extra calories.

vegetable oil cooking spray	1/4 teaspoon nutmeg
3 medium sweet potatoes, peeled	1/4 teaspoon cinnamon
2 tablespoons cooking oil	1/4 teaspoon salt

Preheat oven to 450°. Spray baking pan with cooking spray. Cut each peeled potato lengthwise into 8 wedges. Place potato wedges in a large bowl or zipper-type plastic bag. Add oil and toss. Mix together nutmeg, cinnamon, and salt. Add spice mixture to potato wedges and toss well. Arrange wedges in a single layer on the baking sheet. Bake for 20 to 30 minutes or until tender. Turn potatoes after the first 10 minutes of baking.

187

Serves 4

Nutritional Information per serving:
Calories: 140 • Fat: 7 gm. • Protein: 2 gm.
Carb.: 17 gm. • Cholesterol: 0 • Fiber: low

Sweet Potatoes and Cranberries

This is a real taste treat! Tangy yet sweet.

1 1/2 pounds sweet potatoes,
  cooked or canned

1 1/2 cups raw cranberries

1/2 cup brown sugar

1/2 cup oatmeal, uncooked

1/2 cup butter or margarine, melted

Preheat oven to 350°. Grease a 2-quart casserole dish. Place sliced cooked sweet potatoes in the dish. Layer cranberries, brown sugar, oatmeal, and melted butter on the potatoes. Bake uncovered for 30 minutes.

Serves 8

Nutritional Information per serving:
Calories: 225 • Fat: 11 gm. • Protein: 2 gm.
Carb.: 29 gm. • Cholesterol: 30 mg. • Fiber: medium

188

Zucchini in Light Tomato Sauce

2 tablespoons olive oil
1 pound zucchini, sliced 1/4" thick
2 cloves garlic, minced
14 1/2-ounce can Italian
   tomatoes, chopped
2 tablespoons fresh basil
   or 1 teaspoon dried basil

1/2 teaspoon dried oregano
1 teaspoon sugar
1 tablespoon red wine vinegar
freshly ground pepper and salt
   to taste
4 tablespoons freshly grated
   Parmesan cheese

In a nonstick skillet, heat the olive oil. Add zucchini and cook on high heat, stirring constantly, for 2 minutes. Add garlic. Continue to cook on high heat for 1 minute, stirring to prevent the zucchini from sticking and the garlic from burning. Reduce heat. Add the remaining ingredients except Parmesan cheese. Simmer for 15 minutes. Adjust seasoning with salt and pepper. Serve in small warmed bowls, and top with grated Parmesan cheese.

Note: This can also be refrigerated and served cold as an appetizer or salad. It will thicken slightly when chilled.

For an extra 50 calories per serving, add an extra 2 tablespoons of Parmesan cheese per serving.

Serves 4

Nutritional Information per serving:
Calories: 125 • Fat: 8 gm. • Protein: 4 gm.
Carb.: 10 gm. • Cholesterol: 5 mg. • Fiber: low

Snacks

Apple Muffins

Apple, brown sugar, and cinnamon—a winning combination.

1 egg
1/4 cup oil
2/3 cup milk
1/2 cup sugar
1 1/2 cups flour

1 tablespoon baking powder
1/2 teaspoon salt
1/2 teaspoon cinnamon
1 cup peeled and finely chopped
   apples

Topping

192

1/4 cup brown sugar
1/4 cup chopped nuts

1/2 teaspoon cinnamon

Preheat oven to 400°. Grease muffin tins. In a large bowl, mix egg, oil, and milk. Set aside. In another bowl, combine sugar, flour, baking powder, salt, and cinnamon. Spoon into egg mixture and stir together gently to just mix the ingredients. Mixture will look lumpy. Stir in chopped apples. Spoon into muffin tins, filling half full. To prepare topping, combine brown sugar, nuts, and cinnamon in a small bowl. Sprinkle on muffin batter. Bake for 20 minutes or until light brown. Remove from pan and cool on a rack.

Serves 12

Nutritional Information per serving:
Calories: 175 • Fat: 7 gm. • Protein: 3 gm.
Carb.: 26 gm. • Cholesterol: 15 mg. • Fiber: very low

Apple Pie Cheese Spread

Almost as good as apple pie.

8 ounces fat-free cream cheese, softened

3 tablespoons powdered sugar

1/4 cup vanilla or plain yogurt

2 teaspoons apple pie spice (a mixture of cinnamon, nutmeg, and allspice)

2 tablespoons amaretto

Place all ingredients in a small bowl. Mix with electric mixer until smooth. Add more sugar if you prefer it sweeter. Serve with fresh fruit slices.

For an extra 30 calories per tablespoon, use regular cream cheese.

Serves 20 (1 tablespoon per serving)

Nutritional Information per serving:
Calories: 20 • Fat: 0 • Protein: 2 gm.
Carb.: 3 gm. • Cholesterol: 2 mg. • Fiber: none

193

Apple Raisin Snack Bars

Unbelievably moist.

1 package spice cake mix
3/4 cup light Miracle Whip
2 eggs

1/2 cup peeled and chopped apples
1/2 cup raisins

Frosting

3 1/2 cups powdered sugar
1/2 cup butter or margarine,
  softened

1 tablespoon milk
1 tablespoon brandy (optional)
1 teaspoon vanilla

Preheat oven to 350°. Grease a 9 x 13-inch pan. In a large bowl, combine cake mix, Miracle Whip, and eggs with electric mixer on medium speed until well blended. Stir in apples and raisins. Spread in baking pan. Bake for 25 to 30 minutes or until toothpick inserted in center comes out clean. Cool.

To make frosting: Blend all ingredients with electric mixer until light and fluffy. If frosting is too thick, add extra milk. Spread over bars.

Serves 15

Nutritional Information per serving:
Calories: 375 • Fat: 14 gm. • Protein: 3 gm.
Carb.: 61 gm. • Cholesterol: 40 mg. • Fiber: very low

Bananas with Chocolate Sauce, Nuts, and Wheat Germ

Enjoy high-potassium bananas with your favorite toppings.

4 medium bananas, peeled
1/2 cup chocolate syrup
1/2 cup lightly toasted and
  chopped almonds

1/2 cup wheat germ
1 cup whipped cream (optional)

Place each whole banana in a dessert dish. Top with chocolate syrup, almonds, and wheat germ. Top with whipped cream if desired.

195

Serves 4

Nutritional Information per serving:
Calories: 275 • Fat: 9 gm. • Protein: 6 gm.
Carb.: 49 gm. • Cholesterol: 10 mg. • Fiber: high

Bean Spread

High-protein spread for crackers, chips, or tortillas.
Use any cooked or canned beans of your choice. This high-
protein spread can be served warm or at room temperature.

1/2 cup chopped green onions
3 cloves garlic, minced
2 tablespoons olive oil
30-ounce can white beans, drained

1/4 teaspoon freshly ground pepper
1 tablespoon fresh lemon juice
salt to taste

196

In a medium frying pan, cook onions and garlic in olive oil. Add beans and black pepper, stirring frequently, until heated through. Add lemon juice. Add salt to taste. Mash bean mixture with a potato masher or a food processor. Spread on crackers or warm tortillas.

Serves 20 (2 tablespoons per serving)

Nutritional Information per serving:
Calories: 155 • Fat: 2 gm. • Protein: 10 gm.
Carb.: 26 gm. • Cholesterol: 0 • Fiber: high

Bran Prune Muffins

Unusual muffin that is almost fat free yet moist and tasty.

2 1/2 cups Bran Buds
3/4 cup boiling water
1/2 cup prune puree
1/4 cup molasses
2 cups buttermilk
1 cup sugar

2 eggs
2 1/2 teaspoons baking soda
1 teaspoon salt
1/2 teaspoon cinnamon
2 1/2 cups flour

Preheat oven to 375°. Grease muffin tins. In a small bowl, mix cereal with the boiling water. Set aside. In a large bowl, combine prune puree, molasses, buttermilk, sugar, and eggs. Beat together. Add baking soda, salt, cinnamon, and flour. Stir just until blended. Stir in the moistened cereal. This mixture can be baked immediately or put in a covered bowl in the refrigerator for up to 6 weeks. Fill greased muffin tins 3/4 full. Bake for 15 to 20 minutes or until light brown. Do not overbake.

Note: Prune puree can be purchased or you can make it by blending 4 ounces pitted prunes with 1/4 cup water in a food processor or blender.

Serves 24

Nutritional Information per serving:
Calories: 130 • Fat: 1 gm. • Protein: 4 gm.
Carb.: 30 gm. • Cholesterol: 15 mg. • Fiber: medium

197

Broccoli Dip

Healthy dip to serve with toasted pita
bread wedges, corn chips, or vegetables.

2 cups chopped broccoli
1/4 cup fat-free sour cream
1/4 cup fat-free mayonnaise
1 tablespoon lemon juice

1/4 cup finely chopped red onion
2 tablespoons finely chopped
  fresh herbs*
salt and pepper to taste

198

Cook broccoli until tender. Run under cold water, drain, and pat dry.
Spoon into blender or food processor. Add sour cream, mayonnaise,
and lemon juice. Process until fairly smooth. Stir in onions and herbs.
Add salt and pepper to taste.

*Herbs that are good with this include dill weed, basil, thyme, and tarragon.

To add 100 calories per serving, use regular sour cream and regular
mayonnaise.

Serves 4 (1/2 cup per serving)

Nutritional Information per serving:
Calories: 40 • Fat: 0 • Protein: 2 gm.
Carb.: 8 gm. • Cholesterol: 0 • Fiber: low

Cheese Bread

Make it fast with your favorite cheese.

1 loaf French bread
2 tablespoons extra virgin olive oil
1/2 teaspoon garlic powder
1/4 teaspoon freshly ground
  pepper

1/2 cup grated Parmesan cheese
1 cup grated mozzarella cheese
hot pepper flakes to taste (optional)

Cut a loaf of French bread in half lengthwise. Sprinkle with olive oil. Combine garlic powder, black pepper, and Parmesan cheese in a small bowl. Sprinkle evenly on the bread halves. Sprinkle the mozzarella cheese on the bread. Add red pepper flakes if desired. Broil in oven until light brown and bubbly.

199

Serves 8

Nutritional Information per serving:
Calories: 250 • Fat: 9 gm. • Protein: 11 gm.
Carb.: 30 gm. • Cholesterol: 12 mg. • Fiber: low

Chicken, Pineapple, and Date Spread

A high-protein snack to serve on crackers.

3 cups finely chopped cooked chicken
1 stalk celery, chopped
4 green onions, finely minced
1/2 cup finely chopped dates

1/2 cup pineapple tidbits
1/2 cup fat-free mayonnaise
1 tablespoon honey
1/4 teaspoon seasoned salt
1/2 cup slivered almonds

In a large bowl, combine all ingredients except almonds. Cover and chill. When ready to serve, top with slivered almonds. Check flavor and add more seasoned salt if desired. Serve with crackers. It is attractive if served in a fresh hollowed-out pineapple half.

To add 60 extra calories per serving, use regular mayonnaise.

Serves 12

Nutritional Information per serving:
Calories: 145 • Fat: 5 gm. • Protein: 13 gm.
Carb.: 12 gm. • Cholesterol: 30 mg. • Fiber: low

Chocolate Clusters

You don't even have to bake these.

12 ounces chocolate chips
1/2 cup peanut butter
1 cup dry-roasted peanuts

1 1/2 cups miniature marshmallows
2 cups Rice Krispies

Melt chocolate chips and peanut butter in a large nonstick pan on the very lowest heat, stirring often. Remove from heat and add remaining ingredients. Stir to coat evenly. Drop by the teaspoon onto wax paper or a plate.

201

Serves 40 (1 ball per serving)

Nutritional Information per serving:
Calories: 100 • Fat: 6 gm. • Protein: 2 gm.
Carb.: 9 gm. • Cholesterol: 0 • Fiber: medium

Chocolate Peanut Butter Balls

Have a little chocolate with your oatmeal! So easy—no baking.
Keep these on hand for a quick nutritious treat.

2 cups sugar
1/2 cup butter or margarine
1/2 cup milk
1/4 cup unsweetened cocoa

1/2 cup peanut butter
1 teaspoon vanilla
3 cups quick-cooking oatmeal

Mix sugar, butter, milk, and cocoa in a heavy saucepan. Cook over medium heat, stirring until sugar is melted. Remove from heat and add peanut butter. Stir until melted. Stir in vanilla and oatmeal. Form into small balls and place on wax paper or a plate.

Cool in refrigerator. Place in plastic bag and store in the refrigerator.

Serves 40 (1 ball per serving)

Nutritional Information per serving:
Calories: 105 • Fat: 4 gm. • Protein: 2 gm.
Carb.: 15 gm. • Cholesterol: 5 mg. • Fiber: low

202

Cinnamon Sugar Crunch

A touch of cinnamon and sugar for bite-size treats.
Use any combination of cereals and bite-sized crackers.

3 tablespoons brown sugar

4 tablespoons butter or margarine, melted

1/2 teaspoon ground cinnamon

1 cup crispy corn-rice cereal squares

1 cup whole-grain toasted oat cereal

1 cup bite-sized whole-wheat cereal biscuits

1 cup tiny pretzels, unsalted

1/2 cup raisins (optional)

203

Preheat oven to 350°. Grease a 13 x 9 x 2-inch baking pan. Combine brown sugar and butter in a small saucepan. Stir over low heat until butter is melted. Stir in cinnamon. Combine sugar mixture with cereals and pretzels in the baking pan. Toss gently to coat. Bake for 20 minutes, stirring occasionally. Cool completely. Add raisins if desired. Store in an airtight container.

Serves 4 (1 cup per serving)

Nutritional Information per serving:
Calories: 310 • Fat: 12 gm. • Protein: 4 gm.
Carb.: 46 gm. • Cholesterol: 30 mg. • Fiber: high

Double Corn Muffins

Tasty cornmeal muffins with corn inside.

1 cup cornmeal
1 cup flour
1 tablespoon baking powder
1/2 teaspoon baking soda
2 teaspoons cinnamon
1/2 cup sugar

1/3 cup corn oil
2 eggs
1 cup buttermilk
1 1/2 cups frozen corn
1/2 cup chopped pecans (optional)

Preheat oven to 425°. Grease muffin tins. In a large bowl, mix cornmeal, flour, baking powder, baking soda, cinnamon, and sugar. Make a well in the center. Set aside. In a medium bowl, beat together the oil, eggs, and buttermilk. Stir in the corn and pecans.

Pour this mixture into the center of the dry ingredients and stir until just combined. The mixture will still be lumpy. Fill muffin tins 2/3 full. Bake for 20 minutes or until light brown.

Serves 12

Nutritional Information per serving:
Calories: 220 • Fat: 9 gm. • Protein: 5 gm.
Carb.: 31 gm. • Cholesterol: 30 mg. • Fiber: medium

Granola

Nutritious, delicious, and high-calorie snack.

2 cups old-fashioned oatmeal
1/2 cup shredded coconut
1/2 cup peanuts or chopped
  almonds
1/2 cup wheat germ
1/2 cup sunflower seeds, roasted

1/4 cup sesame seeds (optional)
1 1/2 teaspoons cinnamon
1/4 cup honey or maple syrup
1/4 cup vegetable oil
1 teaspoon vanilla

Dried fruits (optional)

1/2 cup raisins
1/2 cup dried cranberries

1/2 cup dried bananas
1/4 cup diced dried apricot halves

205

Preheat oven to 325°. Lightly oil a baking sheet or spray with cooking spray. Mix oatmeal, coconut, nuts, wheat germ, seeds, and cinnamon in a large bowl. In a separate bowl, mix the honey or maple syrup with the oil and vanilla. Pour the oil mixture over the oatmeal mixture and stir with a large spatula. Spread on the baking sheet. Bake for 25 to 30 minutes until the mixture is roasted, stirring well after the first 15 minutes to be sure the mixture roasts evenly. Add the dried fruits in the last five minutes of roasting. Cool completely and store in an airtight container.

Use as a cereal or as a topping for ice cream, yogurt, pudding, cottage cheese, hot cereal, pancakes, or fresh or canned pears or peaches.

Serves 8

Nutritional Information per serving:
Calories: 350 • Fat: 20 gm. • Protein: 9 gm.
Carb.: 38 gm. • Cholesterol: 0 • Fiber: high

Guacamole

Enjoy it chunky or smooth.

2 medium avocados, ripe but not mushy, cut in 1/2-inch cubes

1 tablespoon extra virgin olive oil

1 tablespoon lime or lemon juice

salt and freshly ground pepper to taste

Optional additional ingredients

minced green onions

minced garlic

minced fresh jalapeño chiles

diced red tomatoes, seeds removed

fresh salsa

fresh cilantro

diced California chiles

green taco sauce

Moisten the chunks of avocado with olive oil and lime or lemon juice. Season with salt and pepper. If desired, add any combination of flavoring ingredients suited to your taste. Serve this guacamole on bread or crackers, on top of chili or black bean soup, as a dip for tortilla chips, or as a side dish salad. Store tightly covered in the refrigerator for up to two days.

For a smooth guacamole, mash the avocado and flavoring with a fork. Use the softer flavoring ingredients such as California chiles or green taco sauce.

Serves 4

Nutritional Information per serving:
Calories: 165 • Fat: 15 gm. • Protein: 2 gm.
Carb.: 6 gm. • Cholesterol: 0 • Fiber: high

Hot Fruit Compote

Attractive, appetizing hot fruit with a tangy taste.
Make ahead and keep refrigerated. Warm it up in
the microwave when you have a taste for it.

12 ounces frozen orange juice
concentrate, thawed

2 tablespoons cornstarch

4 medium apples, cored and
diced

8 ounces pineapple chunks, drained

1 1/2 cups fresh cranberries

6 ounces dried apricot halves

1/4 cup white wine (optional)

207

Preheat oven to 325°. In a small bowl, mix thawed orange juice concentrate with cornstarch. Combine orange juice mixture with all ingredients in large casserole dish with a cover or use aluminum foil for a cover. Bake for 1 hour or until mixture thickens and cranberries are tender.

Serves 10

Nutritional Information per serving:
Calories: 155 • Fat: 0 • Protein: 2 gm.
Carb.: 38 gm. • Cholesterol: 0 • Fiber: high

Hummus

Something a little different—definitely not sweet. This traditional Middle Eastern accompaniment for pita bread is also a good dip for raw vegetables. It is very high in calories and protein.

2 cloves garlic
30 ounces canned garbanzo beans
  (also called chick-peas), drained
1/2 cup tahini (sesame seed paste)
1/2 cup lemon juice

1/3 cup warm water
1/3 cup olive oil
1 teaspoon salt (or to taste)
1/4 teaspoon freshly ground
  pepper (or to taste)

208

Place all ingredients in food processor. Process until smooth. Adjust seasoning. Refrigerate for several hours before serving. Serve at room temperature.

Serves 8 (1/4 cup per serving)

Nutritional Information per serving:
Calories: 570 • Fat: 24 gm. • Protein: 24 gm.
Carb.: 70 gm. • Cholesterol: 0 • Fiber: very high

Lemon Poppy Seed Bread

Super easy way to make a delicious sweet bread.

4 eggs
1 package lemon cake mix
   (with pudding in mix)
3-ounce package instant lemon
   pudding mix

1/2 cup plain yogurt
3 tablespoons poppy seeds
1 cup hot water

Preheat oven to 325°. Grease two large or three small loaf pans. In a large mixing bowl beat eggs. Stir in cake and pudding mixes, yogurt, and poppy seeds. Mix together. Add hot water. Mix well. Pour into loaf pans. Bake for 50 to 60 minutes if using large pans or 40 to 50 minutes if using small pans. Remove loaves from pans.

For an extra 50 calories per serving, substitute cooking oil for the yogurt.

Serves 20

Nutritional Information per serving:
Calories: 150 • Fat: 4 gm. • Protein: 3 gm.
Carb.: 25 gm. • Cholesterol: 35 mg. • Fiber: low

Lemon Zucchini Bread

Add walnuts for extra calories.

3 eggs
1 cup sugar
3/4 cup brown sugar
1 cup vegetable oil
2 teaspoons vanilla extract
1/2 teaspoon lemon extract
1/2 teaspoon baking powder
1 teaspoon baking soda
1 teaspoon salt

2 teaspoons cinnamon
1/2 teaspoon cloves
3 cups flour
2 cups grated zucchini
1 cup golden raisins (optional)
zest of 1 lemon
1 cup toasted and chopped
    walnuts (optional)

210

Preheat oven to 350°. Grease two loaf pans. In a medium bowl, beat eggs. Add sugar, brown sugar, oil, and vanilla and lemon extracts. Beat well. Sift baking powder, baking soda, salt, cinnamon, cloves, and flour together. Gently mix dry ingredients with the egg mixture using as few strokes as possible. Fold in zucchini, raisins, lemon zest, and walnuts. Spoon into loaf pans. Bake for 1 hour or until light brown and wooden pick inserted in the middle comes out clean.

Serves 24 (1 slice per serving)

Nutritional Information per serving:
Calories: 210 • Fat: 10 gm. • Protein: 3 gm.
Carb.: 27 gm. • Cholesterol: 25 mg. • Fiber: low

No-Bake Oatmeal Balls

A high-calorie nibble.

3 cups quick-cooking oatmeal
3/4 cup coconut
1/2 cup chopped toasted walnuts
 or almonds
1/2 cup milk

1/3 cup butter or margarine
1 cup sugar
1/3 cup unsweetened cocoa
1 teaspoon vanilla

In a large bowl, mix oatmeal, coconut, and nuts. In a saucepan, heat milk, butter, and sugar to boiling. Remove from heat. Add cocoa and vanilla. Combine with oatmeal mixture. Stir until blended. Drop from a teaspoon onto wax paper or a plate. Cover and store in the refrigerator.

211

Serves 15 (2 balls per serving)

Nutritional Information per serving:
Calories: 200 • Fat: 9 gm. • Protein: 4 gm.
Carb.: 27 gm. • Cholesterol: 10 mg. • Fiber: medium

Oatmeal Muffins

Wisconsin Governor Tommy Thompson's favorite muffins.

1 cup quick-cooking oatmeal
1 cup buttermilk
1/3 cup butter or margarine
1/2 cup brown sugar
1 egg
2 cups flour

1 teaspoon baking powder
1 teaspoon baking soda
1/2 teaspoon salt
1/4 teaspoon cinnamon (optional)
1/2 cup golden raisins (optional)
cinnamon and sugar (optional)

Preheat oven to 400°. Grease muffin tins. In a small bowl, soak oatmeal in buttermilk. Set aside. In another bowl, beat butter and brown sugar together. Add egg and beat. Mix flour, baking powder, baking soda, salt, and cinnamon. Stir into sugar mixture. Add raisins if desired. Stir in the oatmeal and milk mixture. At this point, the mixture can be stored in the refrigerator for several weeks.

When ready to bake, spoon mixture into muffin pans, filling each tin two-thirds full. Sprinkle top with cinnamon and sugar before baking, if desired. Bake for 20 to 25 minutes or until light brown.

For an extra 25 calories per muffin, add 1 1/2 cups chopped toasted walnuts to the recipe.

Serves 12

Nutritional Information per serving:
Calories: 200 • Fat: 6 gm. • Protein: 4 gm.
Carb.: 32 gm. • Cholesterol: 30 mg. • Fiber: low

Pineapple-Date Dip for Fruit

Serve with fresh strawberries and apple wedges.

1 cup fat-free sour cream
1 cup low-fat whipped topping,
   thawed (e.g. Cool Whip)
1/3 cup chopped pitted dates

8 ounces unsweetened crushed
   pineapple, well drained
1/8 teaspoon ground nutmeg
1/8 teaspoon cinnamon

In a medium bowl, combine sour cream and whipped topping. Stir well. Add dates and pineapple. Stir until well blended. Cover and chill at least 1 hour. Sprinkle with nutmeg and cinnamon.

213

To add 70 calories per serving, use real whipped cream and regular sour cream.

Serves 8 (1/4 cup per serving)

Nutritional Information per serving:
Calories: 80 • Fat: 1 gm. • Protein: 1 gm.
Carb.: 17 gm. • Cholesterol: 5 mg. • Fiber: very low

Salmon Spread

Great snack with crackers.

16-ounce can salmon
8 ounces fat-free cream cheese, softened
1 tablespoon lemon juice

1 tablespoon minced onion
1/2 teaspoon salt
1 tablespoon Worcestershire sauce
1/4 cup chopped parsley

Drain salmon; remove any skin and large bones. In a medium bowl, combine cream cheese, lemon juice, onions, salt, and Worcestershire sauce. Stir in salmon. Cover bowl and chill several hours.

Garnish with chopped parley. Serve on bread or crackers.

To add 70 extra calories per serving, use regular cream cheese.

Serves 8

Nutritional Information per serving:
Calories: 115 • Fat: 3 gm. • Protein: 16 gm.
Carb.: 3 gm. • Cholesterol: 35 mg. • Fiber: very low

214

Six Week Bran Muffins

A great way to have fresh muffins every day.

6 cups All-Bran cereal
2 cups boiling water
1 cup corn oil
3 cups sugar
4 eggs, beaten

1 quart buttermilk
5 cups flour
5 teaspoons baking soda
1 cup toasted walnuts (optional)
1 cup chopped dates (optional)

Preheat oven to 375°. In a medium bowl, combine cereal with boiling water. Set aside. In a large bowl, combine oil, sugar, eggs, and buttermilk. Mix together flour and baking soda and stir into oil mixture. Add the soaked cereal. Stir in nuts and dates if desired. Place in covered jar in the refrigerator. This batter will keep for six weeks in the refrigerator. Do not freeze.

Bake in greased muffin pans for 15 to 20 minutes for small muffins, or 20 to 25 minutes for regular muffins. Bake as many as you want at a time.

Serves 60 (1 small muffin per serving)

Nutritional Information per serving:
Calories: 170 • Fat: 5 gm. • Protein: 4 gm.
Carb.: 27 gm. • Cholesterol: 15 mg. • Fiber: high

215

Soft Granola Bars

You may prefer to substitute chocolate chips for the raisins.
For extra calories, add chocolate frosting.

16 ounces marshmallows

1/2 cup butter or margarine

1/4 cup honey

5 cups Rice Chex cereal, crushed

3 cups quick-cooking oats

1/2 cup graham cracker crumbs

1/2 cup coconut

1/4 cup wheat germ

1 cup raisins

216

Butter a 9 x 13-inch pan. In a large saucepan melt together the marsh-mallows and butter. Add honey and mix well. Remove from heat. Add all remaining ingredients. Mix well. Press into pan. Cut into 20 small squares.

Serves 20

Nutritional Information per serving:
Calories: 235 • Fat: 6 gm. • Protein: 4 gm.
Carb.: 43 gm. • Cholesterol: 12 mg. • Fiber: low

Spanish Peanut Bars

Crunchy high-calorie bars. Great if you like peanuts.

1 1/2 cups flour
3/4 cup brown sugar
1/2 cup butter or margarine,
   melted

6 ounces butterscotch chips
1/2 cup corn syrup
3 tablespoons butter or margarine
2 cups Spanish peanuts

Preheat oven to 350°. Butter a 9 x 13-inch baking pan. In a medium bowl, mix flour, brown sugar, and melted butter together. Pat in baking pan. Bake for 10 minutes.

While this is baking, melt butterscotch chips, corn syrup, and butter together in a nonstick skillet over very low heat. Remove the baking pan from the oven and sprinkle peanuts on the crust. Pour the melted butterscotch mixture over the nuts. Return to oven. Bake about 5 minutes more or just until bubbly. Cut while still warm.

Serves 20 (1 bar per serving)

Nutritional Information per serving:
Calories: 260 • Fat: 14 gm. • Protein: 5 gm.
Carb.: 29 gm. • Cholesterol: 18 mg. • Fiber: medium

Spinach Dip

Serve this spinach dip with raw vegetables for lots of nutrients.

10 ounces chopped frozen
  spinach, thawed
1/2 cup fat-free sour cream
1/2 cup fat-free mayonnaise
1 tablespoon finely chopped
  red onion
1 tablespoon freshly squeezed
  lemon juice

2 cloves garlic, minced
1/4 teaspoon nutmeg
1/4 teaspoon freshly ground pepper
1/4 cup freshly grated Parmesan
  cheese
1/4 cup pine nuts, toasted (optional)

218

Squeeze spinach to remove extra moisture. In a medium bowl, combine the spinach with sour cream, mayonnaise, onions, lemon juice, garlic, nutmeg, pepper, and cheese. Cover bowl and refrigerate for several hours before serving.

Add toasted pine nuts if desired before serving. Serve with crackers, bread sticks, or raw vegetables.

To add 200 extra calories per serving, use regular sour cream and regular mayonnaise.

Serves 6 (1/2 cup per serving)

Nutritional Information per serving:
Calories: 90 • Fat: 4 gm. • Protein: 5 gm.
Carb.: 9 gm. • Cholesterol: 5 mg. • Fiber: high

Spring Garden Dip

Low-fat, high-protein dip.

1 cup plain yogurt, drained
  (yogurt cheese)
1/2 cup low-fat cream cheese,
  softened
1/4 cup grated carrot

1/4 cup minced green onions
1/4 cup finely diced red or green
  bell pepper
2 cloves garlic, minced
salt and freshly ground pepper
  to taste

To make yogurt cheese, place yogurt in a paper coffee filter. Place filter in a strainer over a bowl. Let drain a few hours or overnight in the refrigerator.

In a small bowl, mix yogurt cheese and softened cream cheese. Add all remaining ingredients. Adjust seasoning to taste. Serve with raw vegetables.

219

Serves 4

Nutritional Information per serving:
Calories: 80 • Fat: 5 gm. • Protein: 4 gm.
Carb.: 5 gm. • Cholesterol: 18 mg. • Fiber: low

Desserts

American Apple Crumb Pie

Serve apple pie with cheese and love.

3/4 cup sugar
1/4 cup flour
1/2 teaspoon nutmeg
1/2 teaspoon cinnamon
dash salt

6 cups peeled and thinly sliced
    tart apples
9-inch pie crust, unbaked
2 tablespoons butter or margarine

Topping

1 cup flour
1/2 cup butter or margarine

1/2 cup brown sugar

Preheat oven to 425°. In a large bowl, mix sugar, flour, nutmeg, cinnamon, and salt. Stir in apples. Spoon into an unbaked pie shell. Dot with butter. Set aside. For topping, mix flour, butter, and brown sugar until crumbly. Sprinkle on top of apples. Bake for 50 minutes.

Cover topping with aluminum foil during the last 10 minutes of baking.

Serves 6

Nutritional Information per serving:
Calories: 595 • Fat: 27 gm. • Protein: 5 gm.
Carb.: 83 gm. • Cholesterol: 50 mg. • Fiber: low

Baked Apple Slices

A comforting warm, healthy dessert.

4 large baking apples
3/4 cup sugar
2 teaspoons cinnamon
1/4 teaspoon nutmeg
1/4 teaspoon ginger

1/4 cup apple juice
2 tablespoons butter or margarine
1/2 cup chopped walnuts
ice cream
cinnamon and sugar

Preheat oven to 350°. Butter a small baking dish. Peel apples and cut each apple into 8 slices. Arrange apple slices in the baking dish. In a small bowl, combine sugar, cinnamon, nutmeg, ginger, and apple juice. Pour over apples. Dot with butter. Sprinkle with nuts. Bake uncovered for 45 to 60 minutes or until apples are tender. Serve warm over ice cream. Sprinkle with cinnamon and sugar.

For extra calories, add more butter and nuts and choose a calorie-rich ice cream.

223

Serves 6

Nutritional Information per serving (without ice cream):
Calories 210 • Fat: 5 gm. • Protein: 1 gm.
Carb.: 40 gm. • Cholesterol: 20 mg. • Fiber: medium

Bread Pudding

A warm, comforting dessert. For extra calories,
serve with heavy cream or a custard sauce.

1/3 cup raisins
2 tablespoons brandy
6 thick slices day-old egg bread,
crusts removed
2 tablespoons butter or
margarine softened
1/2 cup brown sugar

1/2 teaspoon cinnamon
1/4 teaspoon nutmeg
3 eggs
1/3 cup sugar
1 teaspoon vanilla
dash salt
2 1/2 cups milk

Preheat oven to 350°. Butter a 9 x 9-inch baking pan or casserole dish.
Soak raisins in brandy for 20 minutes. Drain raisins, saving brandy.
Spread bread with butter. Cut bread into cubes and lightly press into
the pan. Sprinkle with brown sugar, cinnamon, nutmeg, and raisins. In
a small bowl, mix eggs, sugar, vanilla, salt, and milk. Pour over bread.
Place baking dish in a pan of hot water in oven. Bake for 1 hour or until
knife inserted in center comes out clean. Serve warm or cool with
whipped cream. Sprinkle with brandy if desired.

Serves 6

Nutritional Information per serving:
Calories: 310 • Fat: 10 gm. • Protein: 8 gm.
Carb.: 47 gm. • Cholesterol: 115 mg. • Fiber: low

Buttermilk Pie

Some call it sugar pie. An old-fashioned sweet dessert.

1 cup buttermilk
1 1/2 cups sugar
1/2 cup butter or margarine,
  softened

3 eggs
1/4 cup flour
1 teaspoon vanilla
9-inch pie shell, unbaked

Preheat oven to 400°. In a blender or food processor, combine all ingredients except pie shell. Process until smooth. Pour into pie shell. Bake for 20 minutes. Turn down oven temperature to 350° and bake for another 40 minutes.

225

Serves 6

Nutritional Information per serving:
Calories: 525 • Fat: 25 gm. • Protein: 7 gm.
Carb.: 68 gm. • Cholesterol: 135 mg. • Fiber: 0

Chocolate Bavarian

Bavarian has the texture and creaminess of mousse
but it is made without eggs. It is made with heavy cream
and gelatin, and is very high in fat and calories.

2 cups whole milk
1 cup sugar
1/2 cup unsweetened cocoa
1/4 teaspoon salt

1/2 teaspoon vanilla, raspberry,
 or orange extract
1 package unflavored gelatin
2 cups heavy cream

In a non-aluminum saucepan, heat milk with sugar, cocoa, and salt. Stir constantly until cocoa is mixed and the mixture heats thoroughly for 5 minutes. Take off heat and strain. Add the extract. Cool the mixture for 2 hours in the refrigerator.

When the mixture is cooled, dissolve the gelatin in 1/3 cup hot water. Stir until gelatin is completely dissolved. Use additional heat if necessary. Cool slightly. In a chilled bowl, lightly whip the cream with an electric mixer until soft peaks form. Stir the gelatin into the cocoa mixture. Fold in the whipped cream. Pour into a decorative bowl. Refrigerate or freeze.

Serve with delicate cookies, pound cake, angel food cake, or raspberry sauce.

Serves 8

Nutritional Information per serving:
Calories: 400 • Fat: 24 gm. • Protein: 5 gm.
Carb.: 42 gm. • Cholesterol: 90 mg. • Fiber: low

Chocolate Chip Bars

As good as chocolate chip cookies, without all the work.

1 cup butter-flavored shortening
3/4 cup brown sugar
3/4 cup white sugar
2 eggs
1 teaspoon vanilla

2 1/4 cups flour
1 teaspoon baking soda
1 teaspoon salt
12 ounces chocolate chips

Preheat oven to 350°. Butter one 10 x 15-inch baking pan or two 8 x 8-inch pans. In a large bowl, cream shortening and sugars together. Add eggs and vanilla; beat. Combine flour, baking soda, and salt. Stir into the sugar mixture. Add the chocolate chips. Spoon into baking pan. Bake for 15 minutes. Do not overbake.

227

Serves 30 (1 small bar per serving)

Nutritional Information per bar:
Calories: 185 • Fat: 10 gm. • Protein: 2 gm.
Carb.: 22 gm. • Cholesterol: 10 mg. • Fiber: very low

Crème Brûlée

High in calories and rich.

4 egg yolks
1/3 cup sugar
pinch salt

1 teaspoon vanilla
1 1/4 cups heavy cream
1/2 cup brown sugar

Preheat oven to 300°. In a bowl, slightly beat egg yolks. Stir in sugar, salt, and vanilla without creating too many bubbles. In a small saucepan, bring cream to a boil. Remove from heat. Slowly stir into egg mixture. Pour into 6 small custard cups (ramekins). Place cups in a large baking pan. Place the pan on an oven rack. Pour boiling water into the baking pan around the custard cups to a depth of about 1 inch. Bake for 55 to 60 minutes or until a knife inserted near the center comes out clean. When opening the oven door, be careful of the steam produced from the water bath. Remove cups from water. Refrigerate 5 to 6 hours.

When ready to serve, sprinkle the top of each custard with brown sugar. Place under oven broiler until sugar bubbles. Watch carefully. Serve in the custard cups.

Serves 6

Nutritional Information per serving:
Calories: 300 • Fat: 22 gm. • Protein: 3 gm.
Carb.: 23 gm. • Cholesterol: 315 mg. • Fiber: 0

Crème Caramel

A real comfort food—a favorite from the past.

1/3 cup water
1/3 cup sugar
4 eggs
1/3 cup sugar
pinch salt

2 cups milk
1 teaspoon vanilla
zest of 1 lemon or orange
1 tablespoon brandy (optional)

Preheat oven to 300°. Mix water and sugar in a heavy saucepan. Cook over medium heat until sugar dissolves and mixture turns light amber (about 8 to 10 minutes). Quickly divide hot syrup among six custard cups, tilting to coat bottoms. In a bowl, slightly beat eggs with sugar and salt. (Note: Do not create too many bubbles when beating eggs for custard. Bubbles on the surface do not break in the low heat needed to cook the custard.)

229

Heat milk to boiling. Add vanilla and zest. Remove from heat. Slowly pour milk mixture into the egg mixture. Stir while pouring the milk. Pour the mixture through a fine strainer to remove zest. Pour into the custard cups. Place cups in a large baking pan. Place the pan on an oven rack. Pour boiling water into the baking pan around the custard cups to a depth of about 1 inch. Bake for 55 to 60 minutes or until a knife inserted near the center comes out clean. When opening the oven door, be careful of the steam produced from the water bath. Remove cups from water. Cool and refrigerate.

To serve, loosen custard from cups. Invert onto individual serving plates. Sprinkle with brandy if desired.

Serves 4

Nutritional Information per serving:
Calories: 270 • Fat: 8 gm. • Protein: 9 gm.
Carb.: 40 gm. • Cholesterol: 200 mg. • Fiber: 0

Fudge Pie

When you have a taste for something fudgy.

1/3 cup butter or margarine, melted

3 ounces unsweetened baking chocolate

2 cups sugar

4 eggs, beaten

1/4 teaspoon salt

1 teaspoon vanilla

1/2 cup chopped toasted walnuts

Preheat oven to 325°. Butter a 9 x 9-inch pie pan. In a heavy saucepan, melt butter and baking chocolate together over very low heat. Stir in all remaining ingredients. Pour into pan. Bake for 40 to 45 minutes. Pie should appear set around the edges but soft in the middle.

Serve with ice cream or whipped cream topped with raspberry sauce if desired. This dessert freezes well.

Serves 10

Nutritional Information per serving:
Calories: 290 • Fat: 13 gm. • Protein: 3 gm.
Carb.: 43 gm. • Cholesterol: 90 mg. • Fiber: low

Hot Fudge Pudding Cake

So easy—you don't even need a mixing bowl.

1 cup flour
3/4 cup sugar
2 tablespoons unsweetened
  cocoa
2 teaspoons baking powder
1/4 teaspoon salt
1/2 cup milk

2 tablespoons oil
1 teaspoon vanilla
1 cup chopped toasted almonds
  or walnuts
1 cup brown sugar
1/4 cup unsweetened cocoa
1 3/4 cups hot water

231

Preheat oven to 350°. In an ungreased 9 x 9-inch baking pan, mix the flour, sugar, 2 tablespoons cocoa, baking powder, and salt. Stir in the milk, oil, and vanilla until smooth. Stir in nuts. Sprinkle with brown sugar and 1/4 cup cocoa. Pour hot water over batter. Bake for 40 minutes. Cool in pan about 15 minutes. Spoon into dessert dishes. Top with ice cream or whipped cream if desired. This is also good with a raspberry sauce.

Serves 10

Nutritional Information per serving:
Calories: 295 • Fat: 11 gm. • Protein: 5 gm.
Carb.: 44 gm. • Cholesterol: 2 mg. • Fiber: low

Impossible Coconut Pie

Crust forms on the bottom, custard appears in the middle, and coconut rises to the top. Impossible!

2 cups milk	1/2 cup butter or margarine
2/3 cup sugar	1/2 cup flour
4 eggs	1 teaspoon vanilla
1/4 teaspoon salt	1 cup coconut

Preheat oven to 350°. Butter a 10-inch pie pan. Place all ingredients except coconut in a blender or food processor. Process until well mixed. Stir coconut into the mixture. Pour into the pie pan. Bake for 60 minutes. (If glass pan is used, reduce oven temperature to 325°.)

Serves 8

Nutritional Information per serving:
Calories: 280 • Fat: 17 gm. • Protein: 6 gm.
Carb.: 26 gm. • Cholesterol: 130 mg. • Fiber: low

Lemon Bavarian

A creamy, tangy, high-fat and high-calorie dessert.

Lemon Curd

8 ounces unsalted butter,
 cut in cubes
juice and peel of 4 lemons

1 1/2 cups sugar
4 eggs

Bavarian

1 package unflavored gelatin
1/3 cup hot water

2 cups lemon curd
2 cups heavy cream

233

In a non-aluminum saucepan, warm butter, lemon juice, lemon peel, and sugar over low heat until butter is melted. In a small bowl, beat eggs. Whisk eggs into butter-lemon mixture on medium heat. Bring to a boil, stirring constantly. Reduce heat and let mixture simmer for at least 3 minutes. Pour the mixture through a fine strainer. To cool quickly, spread the lemon curd onto a cookie sheet with a rubber spatula and sprinkle lightly with extra sugar. Refrigerate for 1 hour. Lemon curd can be stored in a covered container for at least 7 days.

Dissolve gelatin in 1/3 cup hot water. Stir until gelatin is completely dissolved. Use low heat if necessary. Cool slightly. Mix the gelatin with the lemon curd. In a cold bowl, lightly whip the cream with an electric mixer until soft peaks form. Fold the cream into the lemon mixture. Pour into any decorative bowl. Refrigerate or freeze for at least 2 hours.

Lemon Bavarian can be served with fresh berries, raspberry sauce, or cookies. Lemon curd can be used as a filling for cake layers, spooned over pound cake or angel food cake, spread on muffins, or eaten with delicate cookies.

Serves 12

Nutritional Information per serving:
Calories: 430 • Fat: 30 gm. • Protein: 4 gm.
Carb.: 36 gm. • Cholesterol: 150 mg. • Fiber: 0

Lemon Buttermilk Custard

Smooth, light, and easy to eat.

2 eggs
2/3 cup sugar
1/3 cup flour
2 teaspoons lemon extract

3 cups buttermilk
3 lemons, sliced
1/2 cup blueberries

Preheat oven to 300°. In a small bowl, lightly beat the eggs, and then whisk in sugar and flour. When mixture is smooth, stir in the lemon extract and buttermilk. Pour into 6 custard cups and set them on a baking sheet. Bake for 25 to 35 minutes or until custards are puffed up and set. Cool in the refrigerator.

Serve with lemon slices and blueberries or other fresh fruit.

Serves 6

Nutritional Information per serving:
Calories: 220 • Fat: 3 gm. • Protein: 7 gm.
Carb.: 41 gm. • Cholesterol: 65 mg. • Fiber: very low

Lemon Pudding Cake

Saucy, with fresh lemon flavor.
For extra calories, serve with whipped cream.

2 eggs, separated
1 teaspoon grated lemon peel
1/4 cup fresh lemon juice
1 cup milk

1 cup sugar
1/4 cup flour
1/4 teaspoon salt

Preheat oven to 350°. In a large glass bowl, whip egg whites with an electric mixer until stiff peaks form. Set aside. (Egg whites beat best at room temperature.) In a separate small bowl, beat egg yolks slightly. Add lemon peel, lemon juice, and milk. Add sugar, flour, and salt. Mix until smooth. Fold the beaten egg whites into egg yolk mixture. Pour into ungreased small casserole or an 8 x 8-inch baking dish. Place casserole in a pan of hot water. Bake for 45 to 50 minutes. Be careful of the steam produced from the water when opening the oven door. Serve warm or cool.

235

Serves 6

Nutritional Information per serving:
Calories: 200 • Fat: 3 gm. • Protein: 4 gm.
Carb.: 40 gm. • Cholesterol: 65 mg. • Fiber: 0

Pumpkin Bars

Moist and wonderful. Lots of vitamin A, also.

4 eggs
1 cup vegetable oil
2 cups sugar
16-ounce can pumpkin
2 cups flour
2 teaspoons baking powder

1 teaspoon baking soda
1/2 teaspoon salt
2 teaspoons cinnamon
1/2 teaspoon nutmeg
1/2 teaspoon ginger
1/2 teaspoon cloves

Frosting

8 ounces low-fat cream cheese
1/4 cup butter or margarine
1 teaspoon vanilla

4 cups powdered sugar
1 teaspoon milk, to thin

Preheat oven to 350°. Grease and flour an 11 x 15-inch baking pan or two 9 x 9-inch pans. In a large bowl, combine eggs, oil, sugar, and pumpkin. Mix well. Sift together flour, baking powder, baking soda, salt, and spices. Add the dry ingredients to the pumpkin mixture, and mix together gently. Pour mixture into baking pan. Bake for 25 to 30 minutes. Cool.

To prepare frosting: In a medium bowl, beat together cream cheese, butter, and vanilla with an electric mixer. Add powdered sugar gradually. Beat until light and fluffy. Thin with milk if needed.

Serves 30 (1 bar per serving)

Nutritional Information per serving:
Calories: 250 • Fat: 10 gm. • Protein: 3 gm.
Carb.: 38 gm. • Cholesterol: 30 mg. • Fiber: very low

Quick and Easy Brownies

Soft, gooey brownies—so good, so easy too!

1/3 cup butter or margarine,
  melted
1 cup sugar
1/3 cup unsweetened cocoa
2 eggs, lightly beaten

1/4 teaspoon salt
3/4 cup flour
1/2 teaspoon baking powder
1 teaspoon vanilla

Preheat oven to 350°. Grease an 8 x 8-inch baking pan. In a large saucepan, melt butter. Remove pan from heat and add sugar, cocoa, and beaten eggs. Stir together with a wooden spoon. Stir in salt, flour, baking powder, and vanilla. Spoon into baking pan. Bake for 20 to 25 minutes. Do not overbake. Brownies will appear soft and gooey in the middle.

237

Serves 12 (1 bar per serving)

Nutritional Information per serving:
Calories: 155 • Fat: 6 gm. • Protein: 2 gm.
Carb.: 24 gm. • Cholesterol: 45 mg. • Fiber: very low

Raspberry Kuchen

Remember this one? A taste from the past.

1 cup flour
1/2 teaspoon salt
1/2 cup butter or margarine
2 tablespoons evaporated skim
  milk

1/2 cup flour
1/2 cup sugar
3 cups raspberries, fresh or frozen

Topping

1 cup sugar
1 tablespoon flour
2 eggs, lightly beaten

1 cup evaporated skim milk
1 teaspoon vanilla

Preheat oven to 375°. Butter a 9 x 13-inch baking pan. In a small bowl, combine 1 cup flour and salt. Cut in butter until mixture resembles coarse crumbs. Stir in evaporated milk. Pat into baking pan. In a small bowl, combine 1/2 cup flour and 1/2 cup sugar. Sprinkle over crust. Arrange raspberries over crust. To prepare the topping, combine sugar and flour in a small bowl. Stir in eggs, evaporated skim milk, and vanilla. Pour over berries. Bake for 40 to 45 minutes or until light brown. Serve warm or chilled.

To add 70 calories per serving, use heavy cream instead of evaporated skim milk.

Serves 10

Nutritional Information per serving:
Calories: 320 • Fat: 10 gm. • Protein: 5 gm.
Carb.: 52 gm. • Cholesterol: 60 mg. • Fiber: low

Rhubarb Cobbler

Incredibly delicious and it takes only minutes to make.

4 cups chopped rhubarb, fresh or
  frozen (cut in 1-inch pieces)
1 small package raspberry gelatin
1/3 cup sugar

11-ounce box Jiffy yellow cake mix
1 cup water
1/4 cup butter or margarine

Preheat oven to 325°. Butter a 9 x 11-inch baking pan. Place rhubarb pieces in baking pan. Sprinkle dry gelatin over the rhubarb. Sprinkle sugar on top. Sprinkle the dry cake mix on top. Pour water over mixture. Dot with thin slices of butter. Bake for 45 to 50 minutes or until lightly browned.

239

Serves 12

Nutritional Information per serving:
Calories: 200 • Fat: 6 gm. • Protein: 2 gm.
Carb.: 34 gm. • Cholesterol: 10 mg. • Fiber: very low

Rice Pudding

So comforting—so good!

1/2 cup raisins

2 tablespoons brandy (optional)
  3 large eggs, beaten

2 sticks cinnamon

4 whole cloves

4 cups milk, divided

1/2 cup raw medium grain rice
  or Arborio short grain rice

1/2 teaspoon salt

1 cup sugar

1 teaspoon vanilla

1 teaspoon lemon zest

1/8 teaspoon cardamom (optional)

1/2 cup slivered almonds, toasted
  (optional)

Soak raisins in brandy for 20 minutes, then drain. Tie the cinnamon and cloves in a small, clean piece of cheesecloth. Pour 2 cups of milk in a heavy saucepan. Add the spice bag and heat over low heat. When the milk comes to a boil, slowly stir in the rice. Cook for 30 minutes, stirring occasionally. Remove the spice bag. Continue to cook the rice until it is tender (an additional 15 to 30 minutes).

Preheat oven to 350°. In a separate bowl, mix the remaining 2 cups of milk, salt, sugar, beaten eggs, vanilla, lemon zest, and cardamom. When the rice is tender, remove from heat, and pour the custard mixture over the rice. Gently mix until blended. Add raisins if desired. Pour into a large buttered casserole dish. Set the dish in a pan containing 1 inch of hot water. Bake about 30 minutes or until pudding is set and a knife comes out clean when inserted in the center. Be careful of the steam produced by the water bath when opening the oven door.

Serve warm or chilled. Sprinkle each serving with toasted slivered almonds if desired.

Serves 6

Nutritional Information per serving:
Calories: 445 • Fat: 15 gm. • Protein: 12 gm.
Carb.: 70 gm. • Cholesterol: 110 mg. • Fiber: medium

Silky Raspberry Sauce

Attractive sauce for ice cream, pudding, or angel food cake.

10 ounces frozen raspberries in syrup, thawed

1 teaspoon vanilla
1 teaspoon lemon juice

Drain raspberries, and reserve the syrup. Place raspberries and half the syrup in a blender or food processor. Puree. Press mixture through a strainer. Add vanilla and lemon juice. Stir. Store in the refrigerator for up to 1 week. The extra syrup can be used to thin the sauce.

Serves 6

241

Nutritional Information per serving of sauce:
Calories: 45 • Fat: 0 • Protein: 0
Carb.: 12 gm. • Cholesterol: 0 • Fiber: medium

Sweet Potato Pie

An interesting change from pumpkin pie.
The crust is replaced with chopped nuts.

1 cup finely chopped pecans
or walnuts
2 cups sweet potatoes, mashed
2 eggs
3/4 cup brown sugar

1 1/3 cups evaporated skim milk
1 teaspoon cinnamon
1/2 teaspoon nutmeg
1/2 teaspoon ginger
2 tablespoons rum

242

Preheat oven to 400°. Butter a 9-inch pie pan. Sprinkle chopped nuts evenly in the pan. Set aside. In a large bowl, beat together all remaining ingredients. Pour mixture into pie pan. Bake for 15 minutes and then reduce oven temperature to 350°. Bake for another 35 to 45 minutes or until a knife inserted into the center comes out clean.

Serves 6

Nutritional Information per serving:
Calories: 240 • Fat: 8 gm. • Protein: 7 gm.
Carb.: 34 gm. • Cholesterol: 60 mg. • Fiber: low

Soft, Chopped, or Pureed Diet

The following hints and recipes have been contributed by those who
have had problems chewing and swallowing regular foods. Through
trial and error, we have discovered ways to prepare tasty soft, chopped,
or pureed foods.

Hints

❖ Any food can be chopped or pureed in a food processor except
for cooked potatoes (makes the potatoes a sticky consistency)
and raw onions (tears the membranes of the onions, releasing
their juices and making them too strong).

❖ Process foods to the consistency that works best for you.

❖ Keep a small amount of the food out of the food processor or
blender. Place that whole food on your plate next to the
chopped or pureed food. Looking at the whole food before it is
pureed may make your plate more attractive and make your meal
more appealing. At least you will be reminded of what you are
really eating!

❖ It is important to prepare and season the foods to make them
both smell and taste as appealing as regular foods.

❖ A good food processor is needed. A blender does not work well
for all foods unless there is sufficient liquid.

❖ An important safety tip to remember when blending hot foods:
Do not fill the blender or food processor more than one-half full
of hot foods or hot liquids. Place a towel over the top and pulsate
several times to prevent the top from popping off due to hot
steam.

❖ Freeze any leftovers in small plastic freezer bags or covered containers. Meals can be safely frozen without loss of flavor for up to
six months.

❖ Potatoes do not freeze well. Add cooked fresh potatoes to recipes just before serving.

❖ Potatoes and dried potato flakes can be used as thickening agents in soups and stews.

❖ Packaged gravy mixes are easy to use. Gravy adds flavor and moisture when pureeing meats.

❖ Infuse soups and stews with flavor without adding the actual herb or spice to the food by placing whole herbs and spices in a cheesecloth package tied with string. This acts as a flavoring packet (bouquet garni). Remove and discard the packet after cooking.

❖ Experiment with different spices, herbs, and marinades to add zest to your recipe creations. Use sauces and accompaniments on the pureed food or add them to the cooked foods before being pureed.

Flavor your foods with the following suggestions:

Beef: dry mustard, sage, marjoram, rosemary, thyme, basil, oregano, chili powder, cayenne, Worcestershire sauce, parsley, shallots, garlic

Lamb: garlic, rosemary, parsley, capers, or mint sauce or mint jelly as an accompaniment after cooking

Pork: soy sauce, ginger, onions, garlic, shallots, honey, mustard; fruit juices, and vinegar for marinades and basting; chutney or mild green chili sauce as an accompaniment to roasted pork; crumbled sage and ground fennel seed in ground pork

Poultry: garlic, onions, shallots, parsley, thyme, saffron, curry powder, marjoram, ginger, rosemary, fresh tarragon

Fish: garlic, shallots, thyme, dill weed, fresh tarragon, basil, capers

Eggs: garlic, chives, dry or prepared mustard, curry powder, paprika, turmeric, basil, fresh tarragon, fresh chervil

Rice: curry, saffron, cinnamon

Fruit: mint, honey, cinnamon, ginger; poach in fruit juice and brandy with finely minced lemon or orange zest along with a cinnamon stick, star anise, and whole cloves

Red wine complements beef recipes.

White wine complements poultry recipes.

Dry white sherry complements seafood recipes.

Enjoy any wine that tastes good to you.

Soups

❖ Any soup can easily be pureed. Some vegetable soups such as asparagus soup may need to be strained if there is excess stringy fiber.

❖ Puree any canned or homemade bean or pea soup. Thin with chicken or beef broth.

Meat, Poultry, and Fish

❖ Prepare well-done meat, poultry, and fish using your favorite recipe. Process meat with broth. Add cooked potatoes or other vegetables to thicken the mixture and to add extra flavor and nutrients.

❖ The food processor chops or purees your favorite stews and casseroles to your desired consistency.

❖ If you do not have mouth sores, try pureed canned mild chili con carne. Thin with beef stock. Serve with rice.

❖ Try eating canned tamales with the gravy. After removing the corn husks, the tamales can be eaten as they are, mashed with a fork, or pureed. The fillings in commercially prepared tamales are usually ground meat products.

❖ Try eating deviled ham salad or tuna salad by adding extra mayonnaise to your favorite recipe or a commercial product.

❖ For extra protein, process your main course dishes with added tofu. The tofu has no flavor of its own but adds nutrients and a smooth consistency.

Eggs

❖ Make creamy egg salad by finely chopping hard cooked eggs, and adding mayonnaise, whipping cream, mustard, garlic powder, salt, and pepper. For a variation, add curry powder or finely minced chives.

❖ Scramble eggs with extra milk. Add grated cheese near the end of the cooking process to make a creamier egg dish.

Starches and Cereals

❖ Mash potatoes using a whisk, electric mixer, ricer, or masher. (A food processor will create sticky, glue-like potatoes.) Add hot milk or cream and butter until the desired consistency is obtained. Season with salt and pepper. For extra calories, add lots of butter.

❖ Make mashed potato salad by mashing cooked, peeled potatoes. Add finely chopped hard cooked eggs, mayonnaise, prepared mustard, salt, ground pepper, garlic, and onion powder. Add mayonnaise until the mixture is creamy. A small amount of white wine vinegar gives the salad a tart taste. Chill and serve cold.

❖ Cook rice or small pasta varieties (stars, ditalini, pastina) in chicken or beef broth. Add seasonings such as salt, pepper, or a favorite herb or spice to taste. Add extra liquid for cooking the rice or pasta to make a dish that is easy to swallow.

❖ Cook instant grits according to package directions. Add butter and grated cheese. Use chicken stock to thin. Season with black pepper, salt, garlic powder, and paprika. Thoroughly heat or bake for 20 minutes at 350°. Serve with extra cheese on top.

❖ Puree drained, canned white beans with finely minced garlic, lemon juice, olive oil, parsley, salt, and pepper. This is usually spread on bread or used as a dip for vegetables but can also be eaten as a side dish.

❖ Puree refried beans with chicken or beef broth to thin. Heat to warm. Flavor with mild green chili sauce. Add cheese for extra protein and calories.

❖ Make hummus by pureeing garbanzo beans with olive oil, finely minced garlic, lemon juice, freshly ground pepper, salt, and tahini paste (sesame seed paste).

Fruits and Vegetables

❖ All canned fruits are easy to puree. Place fruits in the food processor without the syrup and add syrup back to make the desired consistency.

❖ Fresh fruits can be processed with a small amount of lemon juice or orange juice concentrate to keep the color bright. Add sugar to taste.

❖ Make your own applesauce by stewing large chunks of peeled apples in apple juice with a cinnamon stick and whole cloves until the apples are soft. Remove the cinnamon stick and cloves. Mash with a fork. Add butter, vanilla extract, and ground cinnamon to taste. Brandy can be added if desired.

❖ Raspberry sauce is made by pureeing frozen raspberries in heavy syrup, straining out the seeds, and adding a small amount of vanilla extract. Orange or almond extract can be added to give it an exotic flavor. Strawberry sauce is made the same way, except there is no need to strain the seeds.

❖ Prepare sorbet by processing canned fruits or frozen berries in heavy syrup. Freeze the mixture in shallow containers. Stir once or twice during the freezing process. Raspberries or blackberries should be strained before freezing to remove seeds.

❖ Fruit slushies are easy to prepare by processing a combination of any of the following fruits: bananas, kiwis, mangoes, papayas, canned pears or peaches, strawberries, or melon. Process the fruits with a handful of ice cubes and any fruit juice, such as apple, orange, cranberry, pear, or apricot nectar. For a thinner slushy, add more juice. For a more creamy slushy, use a banana. If you have sores in your mouth, process the fruit with apple juice, apricot, or pear nectar. You may add a little sugar for extra sweetness.

❖ Cooked and canned vegetables can be processed. Some vegetables need to be peeled before cooking, including the stalks of broccoli and asparagus. If excess fiber remains in the pureed mixture, you may need to strain it. Add enough liquid to make the desired consistency.

❖ Mash avocado with a fork. Add lemon juice and mayonnaise or sour cream. Add salt, pepper, and garlic powder to taste. Eat as a side dish or mix with cooked ground beef, turkey, or chicken.

Desserts

❖ Mix canned fruits in their juices with instant pudding mix.

❖ Prepare pudding or mousse from packaged instant mixes. Layer pudding or mousse with sweetened whipped cream in a tall glass. Top with your favorite ice cream syrup.

❖ Prepare packaged cheesecake mixes without using the crust. Press the mixture into a buttered pan. When set, eat with raspberry or strawberry fruit sauce with a dollop of sweetened whipped or sour cream.

❖ Try jellied cranberry sauce with whipped cream or sour cream topping for a not so sweet dessert.

❖ Cook rice or hot cereal, such as Cream of Wheat, Cream of Rice, or Malt-o-Meal, according to package directions. After the rice or cereal is cooked, add honey or maple syrup, cinnamon, hot milk, and butter for a rich, creamy dessert or midday snack.

247

❖ Try apple pie and ice cream in the food processor.

❖ Thin desserts in the food processor with milk, cream, frozen whipped topping, yogurt, sour cream, chocolate or caramel sauce, fruit, juice, etc.

Broccoli Soup

1 leek, chopped
1 small onion, diced
1 carrot, diced
2 cloves garlic, minced
2 tablespoons butter or margarine
4 cups chicken stock

1 medium potato, finely chopped
1 head broccoli, chopped
1 cup milk
1/4 teaspoon cayenne pepper
1/4 teaspoon freshly ground pepper
salt to taste

In a large saucepan, cook the leek, onions, carrots, and garlic in butter until onions are translucent. Add chicken stock, potatoes, and broccoli. Bring to a boil. Reduce heat and simmer until vegetables are tender. Add milk and seasonings. Heat through. Pour soup into food processor and process until smooth. Adjust seasonings to taste.

To add an additional 140 calories per serving, substitute heavy cream for the milk.

Serves 5

Nutritional Information per serving:
Calories: 140 • Fat: 7 gm. • Protein: 7 gm.
Carb.: 12 gm. • Cholesterol: 13 mg. • Fiber: low

249

Carrot Soup with Ginger

Subtle flavors of lemon, curry, and ginger.

2 tablespoons butter or margarine
2 medium onions, diced
2 stalks celery, diced
2 cloves garlic, minced
1/4 teaspoon curry powder
1/4 teaspoon ground ginger
2 pounds carrots, peeled and sliced

4 cups chicken stock
1 teaspoon salt
1/4 teaspoon black pepper
1 teaspoon lemon juice
1/4 cup evaporated skim milk
cayenne pepper
sour cream for garnish

In a large soup pot, melt the butter on low heat. Add the onions, celery, garlic, curry powder, and ginger. Cook the vegetables on low heat until the onions are translucent. Add carrots, chicken stock, salt, and pepper. Bring to a boil, then reduce heat. Simmer until the carrots are soft enough to puree (30 to 40 minutes). Add the lemon juice. Let cool slightly. Puree the mixture in batches using a blender or food processor. Return the mixture to the soup pot. Whisk in the milk until thoroughly mixed. Reheat gently, but do not boil. Adjust seasoning with salt and pepper. Add extra milk to thin if desired. Serve with a dash of cayenne pepper and a dollop of sour cream if desired.

For an extra 60 calories per serving, substitute 1/2 cup of heavy cream for the 1/4 cup of evaporated skim milk.

Serves 6

Nutritional Information per serving:
Calories: 140 • Fat: 5 gm. • Protein: 6 gm.
Carb.: 18 gm. • Cholesterol: 20 mg. • Fiber: high

Chicken Soup—Pureed

Soup the easy way. Add more chicken for
extra protein. Add any vegetables of your choice.

1 1/2 cups chicken stock
1 stalk celery, diced
1 medium carrot, diced
1 medium potato, diced
pinch dried thyme

1/2 cup cooked chicken
10-ounce can chicken soup of
   your choice
freshly ground pepper to taste

In a medium saucepan, heat the chicken stock to a boil. Add the celery,
carrot, potato, and thyme. Reduce heat, and simmer until vegetables are
done. Add the chicken and canned soup. Heat thoroughly. Pour in a
blender or food processor. Process until smooth. Serve with freshly
ground pepper.

251

Serves 2

Nutritional Information per serving:
Calories: 210 • Fat: 7 gm. • Protein: 19 gm.
Carb.: 16 gm. • Cholesterol: 40 mg. • Fiber: low

Crab Bisque

1 medium onion, minced
1 tablespoon butter or margarine
1 tablespoon flour
4 cups milk
10-ounce can tomato soup

12 ounces surimi seafood or crabmeat
salt and freshly ground pepper
 to taste
1/4 cup sherry

In a heavy saucepan on low heat, cook onion in butter until translucent. Add flour and cook 5 minutes, stirring constantly. Add milk and tomato soup. Cook over medium heat for 10 minutes. Add surimi or crab and heat thoroughly. Season to taste. Stir in sherry just before serving. Process in food processor if desired.

To add an additional 160 calories per serving, substitute half and half for the milk.

Serves 4

Nutritional Information per serving:
Calories: 330 • Fat: 13 gm. • Protein: 23 gm.
Carb.: 30 gm. • Cholesterol: 65 mg. • Fiber: very low

252

Hearty Vegetable Soup

Wonderful homemade flavor.

3 tablespoons butter or margarine
2 medium onions, diced
2 large carrots, diced
3 stalks celery, diced
1 clove garlic, finely minced
2 cups shredded cabbage
4 medium potatoes, peeled
  and diced
2 medium parsnips, peeled
  and sliced

1 quart beef or chicken broth
1 cup frozen green peas
1/2 cup V-8 vegetable juice
  or tomato juice
2 tablespoons minced fresh parsley
salt and freshly ground pepper
  to taste
cayenne pepper to taste

253

Heat butter in a heavy saucepan. Add onions, carrots, celery, and garlic. Cook until the onions are translucent. Do not brown. Add the cabbage, potatoes, parsnips, and broth. Bring to a boil. Reduce heat and simmer until the potatoes and parsnips are cooked, about 30 minutes. Add the peas, vegetable juice, and parsley. Cook for 3 to 5 minutes. Season with salt and pepper. Pour mixture into food processor and process until smooth, if desired. Serve with Parmesan cheese if desired.

Serves 6

Nutritional Information per serving:
Calories: 225 • Fat: 8 gm. • Protein: 12 gm.
Carb.: 29 gm. • Cholesterol: 15 mg. • Fiber: high

Pastina Vegetable Soup

An unusual mild comfort soup.

3 tablespoons butter or margarine
1 medium onion, finely minced
2 stalks celery, finely diced
1 medium carrot, finely diced
2 cloves garlic, finely minced
1 clove shallot, finely minced
4 cups chicken stock
1/2 cup dried pastina pasta
1/4 teaspoon freshly grated
   nutmeg

2 tablespoons minced fresh
   parsley
1/2 teaspoon freshly ground
   pepper
1 tablespoon lemon juice
salt and pepper to taste
4 tablespoons freshly grated
   Parmesan cheese

Melt the butter in a heavy saucepan. Add the onion, celery, carrots, garlic, and shallots. Cook over low heat until onions are translucent. Add the chicken stock; bring to a boil. Add the pasta. Bring to a boil, then turn heat down and simmer until the pasta is just cooked (7 to 8 minutes). Add the nutmeg, parsley, black pepper, and lemon juice. Simmer an additional 2 to 3 minutes. Season with salt and additional pepper to taste. Serve with Parmesan cheese.

For an additional 50 calories per serving, add an additional 1/2 cup grated Parmesan cheese to the recipe.

Serves 4

Nutritional Information per serving:
Calories: 215 • Fat: 12 gm. • Protein: 10 gm.
Carb.: 18 gm. • Cholesterol: 30 mg. • Fiber: low

Peanut Carrot Soup

High calories and protein. Rich in vitamin A.

2 tablespoons butter or margarine
2 cups peeled, diced carrots
2 stalks celery, diced
1 medium onion, chopped

4 cups chicken broth
1/3 cup creamy peanut butter
1/2 cup heavy cream
salt and pepper to taste

In a heavy saucepan, melt the butter and cook carrots, celery, and onion in butter until onions are tender. Add broth, and stir constantly until mixture comes to a boil. Reduce heat and simmer until carrots are tender, about 15 minutes. Add peanut butter and cream but do not boil. Puree in blender or food processor. Add seasonings to taste. Return to pan to heat. Thin with extra broth if soup is too thick.

255

Serves 4

Nutritional Information per serving:
Calories: 390 • Fat: 30 gm. • Protein: 18 gm.
Carb.: 14 gm. • Cholesterol: 60 mg. • Fiber: medium

Potato Soup

Plain and simple.

2 tablespoons butter or margarine
1 large onion, chopped
2 large carrots, chopped
4 stalks celery, chopped
2 cloves garlic, minced
3 large potatoes, peeled and cubed

4 cups chicken broth
1/2 pound cooked ham, cubed
  (optional)
1 cup milk
1/4 teaspoon white pepper
salt to taste

256

Heat butter in a large saucepan. Add the onions, carrots, celery, and garlic. Cook until onion is translucent. Add the potatoes and chicken broth. Bring to a boil, reduce heat, and simmer for 30 to 40 minutes or until potatoes are tender. Add ham if desired. Place soup mixture in food processor. Process until smooth. Return pureed soup to cooking pot. Add milk. Gently heat but do not boil. Season with salt and pepper. Thin soup with warm chicken broth if it gets too thick. Heat and serve.

To add 200 extra calories per serving, substitute half and half for the milk and add 2 cups shredded Swiss cheese to the recipe.

Serves 6

Nutritional Information per serving:
Calories: 230 • Fat: 11 gm. • Protein: 17 gm.
Carb.: 16 gm. • Cholesterol: 40 mg. • Fiber: low

Sweet Cream of Pea Soup

A soup that tastes as good cold as hot.

1 medium onion, diced
1 clove garlic, minced
2 tablespoons butter
1 carrot, sliced
2 medium potatoes, peeled
  and sliced

2 cups frozen peas
3 cups chicken stock, divided
2 cups milk, warmed
salt and freshly ground pepper
  to taste

In a heavy saucepan, cook onion and garlic in butter until onions are translucent. Add the carrots, potatoes, peas, and 2 cups stock. Bring to a boil. Reduce heat, cover, and simmer for about 30 minutes until vegetables are tender. Spoon vegetables into a blender or food processor; process until smooth. Pour back into saucepan and combine with remaining broth. Add milk to desired consistency. Adjust seasonings to taste. May be served hot or cold.

To add an additional 80 calories per serving, substitute half and half for the milk. To add an additional 330 calories per serving, substitute heavy cream for the milk.

257

Serves 4

Nutritional Information per serving:
Calories: 260 • Fat: 11 gm. • Protein: 13 gm.
Carb.: 27 gm. • Cholesterol: 30 mg. • Fiber: high

Fluffy Dilled Carrots and Potatoes

2 cups sliced carrots
1 cup sliced potatoes
1/4 cup skim milk
2 tablespoons butter or margarine

1/4 teaspoon salt
dash white pepper
1/4 teaspoon dill weed
1/4 teaspoon onion powder

In a saucepan, cook carrots and potatoes in boiling water until tender. Drain. Add remaining ingredients and beat with electric mixer until smooth. Add extra milk to thin if needed. Reheat before serving.

To add an additional 120 calories per serving, substitute heavy cream for the skim milk and add 2 tablespoons butter to the recipe.

Serves 4

Nutritional Information per serving:
Calories: 95 • Fat: 6 gm. • Protein: 2 gm.
Carb.: 8 gm. • Cholesterol: 15 mg. • Fiber: low

258

Mashed Sweet Potatoes

2 pounds sweet potatoes
2 tablespoons butter, softened
1/2 cup milk, warmed
1/2 teaspoon salt

1/2 teaspoon freshly ground pepper
1/4 teaspoon ground ginger
 (optional)
brown sugar to taste

In a large saucepan, cook sweet potatoes until tender. Drain. Peel potatoes. Place sweet potatoes in a large bowl. Mash with a masher or an electric mixer. Add butter, warm milk, salt, pepper, and ginger. Mash until light and creamy. Add extra milk to thin if desired. May be rewarmed in a microwave. Add a small amount of brown sugar for extra sweetness if desired.

To add an additional 150 calories per serving, add 3 tablespoons of butter to the recipe and substitute heavy cream for the evaporated milk.

259

Serves 4

Nutritional Information per serving:
Calories: 240 • Fat: 7 gm. • Protein: 4 gm.
Carb.: 41 gm. • Cholesterol: 20 mg. • Fiber: high

Potato Duchesse

A classic French potato side dish.
This is good if you need extra calories.

1 1/2 cups mashed potatoes
1/4 cup milk
2 eggs
1/4 cup grated Parmesan cheese

1/2 cup shredded Swiss cheese
2 tablespoons fresh minced parsley
1 teaspoon salt
1/2 teaspoon white pepper

Line a cookie sheet with parchment paper or spray with cooking spray. Mix all ingredients together. If you have a piping bag, use a star tip to pipe swirls of potato mixture onto the cookie sheet. If you do not have a piping bag, use an ice cream scoop to make small mounds of potatoes, and rake the surface with a fork. Refrigerate for 30 minutes.

Preheat oven to 325°. Bake until brown, about 30 to 40 minutes.

Serves 4

Nutritional Information per serving:
Calories: 200 • Fat: 9 gm. • Protein: 12 gm.
Carb.: 18 gm. • Cholesterol: 110 mg. • Fiber: very low

Squash and Carrot Puree

1 medium butternut squash,
  peeled and cubed
4 large carrots, peeled and cubed
1 cup chicken stock
2 tablespoons sherry

2 tablespoons brown sugar
1/4 teaspoon nutmeg or ginger
1/4 teaspoon white pepper
1 teaspoon salt
2 tablespoons butter or margarine

In a saucepan, simmer squash and carrots in chicken broth until fork tender. Add all remaining ingredients. Simmer an additional 3 to 5 minutes. Process in food processor until smooth. Adjust seasoning. Transfer to serving bowl.

261

To add an additional 100 calories per serving, increase butter to 1/2 cup.

Serves 6

Nutritional Information per serving:
Calories: 120 • Fat: 4 gm. • Protein: 2 gm.
Carb.: 19 gm. • Cholesterol: 10 mg. • Fiber: low

Vegetable Cream Puree

4 cups diced vegetables of your
  choice
2 cups chicken broth
1 tablespoon butter or margarine
1 tablespoon flour

1 cup skim milk
1/4 teaspoon white pepper
1/4 teaspoon nutmeg
salt to taste

In a large saucepan, cook vegetables in chicken broth until tender. Remove vegetables, saving the broth for other use. Set vegetables aside. Melt butter in heavy saucepan. Stir in flour and cook for at least 5 minutes. Add milk and seasonings. Cook over low heat until thickened. Add more chicken broth to thin the sauce if it is too thick. Stir in the cooked vegetables. Pour into blender or food processor. Process until smooth.

To add an additional 180 calories per serving, substitute heavy cream for the skim milk.

Serves 4

Nutritional Information per serving:
Calories: 135 • Fat: 4 gm. • Protein: 9 gm.
Carb.: 15 gm. • Cholesterol: 10 mg. • Fiber: medium

262

Braised Chicken—Pureed

Frying the chicken adds more flavor.

2 chicken breast halves skinless
  and boneless
1 tablespoon butter or margarine

2 cups chicken broth
1 large potato, chopped
salt and pepper to taste

In a heavy frying pan, brown chicken in butter. Add broth and potatoes. Cover pan and simmer for about 45 minutes or until chicken and potatoes are tender. Check frequently and add extra broth if it gets too dry. Place in blender or food processor and process until smooth. Add salt and pepper to taste.

263

Serves 2

Nutritional Information per serving:
Calories: 280 • Fat: 10 gm. • Protein: 38 gm.
Carb.: 10 gm. • Cholesterol: 80 mg. • Fiber: very low

Roast Beef

Roast your meat with the seasoning of your choice.

2 pounds chuck roast
1/2 teaspoon salt
1/2 teaspoon pepper
10-ounce can cream of
  mushroom soup
1/2 cup water

4 medium potatoes, peeled and
  chopped
4 medium carrots, peeled and
  chopped
beef broth, to thin

264

Preheat oven to 325°. Sprinkle salt and pepper over meat. Place in heavy roasting pan and cover with canned soup. Add water, potatoes, and carrots. Cover pan and bake 2 to 3 hours or until meat is tender. Place meat, vegetables, and juices in food processor and process until smooth. Add beef broth to thin for the desired consistency.

Serves 6

Nutritional Information per serving:
Calories: 400 • Fat: 26 gm. • Protein: 26 gm.
Carb.: 16 gm. • Cholesterol: 90 mg. • Fiber: low

Round Steak—Pureed

1 pound round steak
1/4 cup flour
1/2 teaspoon salt
1/2 teaspoon pepper
1 small onion, chopped
2 tablespoons cooking oil

1 tablespoon tomato paste
1/2 cup red wine
2 cups beef broth
1 tablespoon Worcestershire sauce
  or steak sauce
salt and pepper to taste

Cut round steak into cubes. Combine flour, salt, and pepper. Place flour mixture in a bag. Add meat pieces and shake until meat is coated. Set aside. In a heavy frying pan, cook onions in oil until translucent. Add meat pieces and fry until brown. Add remaining ingredients and bring to a boil, stirring constantly, to make a sauce. Reduce heat, cover, and simmer for about 2 hours or until meat is tender. Check frequently and add extra broth if it gets too dry.

265

Season to taste with extra salt and pepper. Place meat and sauce in food processor. Process until desired consistency. Freeze extra servings.

Serves 4

Nutritional Information per serving:
Calories: 360 • Fat: 22 gm. • Protein: 29 gm.
Carb.: 11 gm. • Cholesterol: 70 mg. • Fiber: low

Steak and Mushrooms—Pureed

1 pound sliced tenderloin beef
1 tablespoon butter or margarine
1/2 pound fresh mushrooms,
 sliced

2 large potatoes, boiled, peeled,
 and sliced
1 cup hot beef broth, to thin
salt and pepper to taste

In a heavy frying pan, sauté slices of tenderloin in butter until brown. Add fresh mushrooms and cook until soft. Combine meat, mushrooms, and potatoes in blender or food processor. Process until smooth. Add heated beef broth to thin. Add seasonings to taste. Freeze extra servings.

266

Serves 4

Nutritional Information per serving:
Calories: 410 • Fat: 30 gm. • Protein: 25 gm.
Carb.: 11 gm. • Cholesterol: 90 mg. • Fiber: low

Steak and Peppers—Pureed

Add extra seasoning to suit your taste.

1 pound round steak or chuck roast
1 medium onion, chopped
2 tablespoons cooking oil
1 medium red pepper, chopped
1 medium yellow pepper, chopped

15-ounce can chopped tomatoes
1 tablespoon steak or chili sauce
1/2 cup beef broth
salt and freshly ground pepper
to taste

Cut meat into cubes. In a heavy pan, brown meat and onions in oil. Add all remaining ingredients. Bring to a boil. Reduce heat, cover and simmer for 2 hours or until meat is tender. Check frequently and add extra broth if it gets too dry.

267

Season with additional salt and pepper if desired. Place meat, vegetables, and sauce in batches in blender or food processor. Process to desired consistency. Freeze extra servings.

Serves 4

Nutritional Information per serving:
Calories: 330 • Fat: 21 gm. • Protein: 25 gm.
Carb.: 10 gm. • Cholesterol: 70 mg. • Fiber: medium

Turkey with Gravy

Use leftover turkey.

1 small onion, finely chopped
1 tablespoon butter
1 tablespoon flour
1 teaspoon poultry seasoning

1 cup chicken broth
1 pound skinless turkey or chicken
    breast meat, cooked and diced
salt and freshly ground pepper to taste

In a heavy saucepan on low heat, cook onions in butter until onions are translucent. Add flour and cook, stirring, for 5 minutes. Add poultry seasoning and chicken broth. Bring to a boil, stirring constantly. Reduce heat and cook until mixture thickens, about 5 minutes. Add turkey pieces. Heat thoroughly. Add salt and pepper to taste. Process in a blender or food processor to desired consistency. Add extra broth to thin as needed.

Serves 4

Nutritional Information per serving:
Calories: 160 • Fat: 5 gm. • Protein: 24 gm.
Carb.: 4 gm. • Cholesterol: 60 mg. • Fiber: very low

Beverages

Bucky Badger Punch

Tangy and not too sweet. Use regular 7-Up for extra calories.

1 quart cranberry juice cocktail   1 cup orange juice
1 cup grapefruit juice   2 cups diet 7-Up or club soda

Combine the 3 juices in a pitcher. Add 7-Up or club soda when ready
to serve.

Serves 8

Nutritional Information per serving:
Calories: 100 • Fat: 0 • Protein: 0.5 gm.
Carb.: 24 gm. • Cholesterol: 0 • Fiber: very low

270

Delicious High-Calorie Malt

Wow—great taste and lots of calories. It is creamy, thick, and
very tasty. Change the flavors and ingredients to suit your taste.

1/2 cup whole milk   1 tablespoon malted milk powder
1/2 cup half and half   1-ounce package instant breakfast
2 cups ice cream, any flavor   powder, any flavor
2 tablespoons Ovaltine

Mix all ingredients together in a food processor. Process until smooth.
Drink immediately. Save any extra in the freezer.

Serves 1

This malt provides 1000 to 1300 calories, depending on the ice cream you choose.

Nutritional Information per serving:
Calories: 1100 • Fat: 48 gm. • Protein: 26 gm.
Carb.: 140 gm. • Cholesterol: 180 mg. • Fiber: 0

Fresh Citrus Cooler

Refreshing drink when extra fluids are needed.
For extra calories, use regular 7-Up in place of club soda.

1 cup fresh orange juice
1/2 cup fresh lemon juice
1/2 cup fresh lime juice

1/3 cup sugar
1 cup club soda, chilled
lime wedges (optional)

Combine first 4 ingredients in a pitcher. Stir until sugar dissolves. Add chilled club soda. Add extra club soda for a lighter taste. Serve over ice. Garnish with lime wedges.

Serves 3

Nutritional Information per serving:
Calories: 155 • Fat: 0 • Protein: 1 gm.
Carb.: 38 gm. • Cholesterol: 0 • Fiber: very low

271

High-Protein Milk

Drink this fortified milk or use it in cooking for extra protein.

1 quart whole milk

1/2 cup dry skim milk powder

With a wire whip or electric mixer, mix the whole milk with the dry skim milk powder until smooth. Chill for at least 4 hours for better taste. Store in the refrigerator.

For an extra 150 to 300 calories per serving, add 1/2 cup of ice cream to each serving.

Serves 4

Nutritional Information per serving:
Calories: 200 • Fat: 8 gm. • Protein: 14 gm.
Carb.: 18 gm. • Cholesterol: 35 mg. • Fiber: 0

Island Tea

Keep on hand for afternoon tea.

1 orange
2 cups water
2 cups pineapple-orange juice

2 tablespoons finely chopped
crystallized ginger
4 tea bags, decaffeinated

Remove the rind from the orange. Set aside the rind. Cut orange in half and squeeze juice from halves. Combine the orange rind, fresh-squeezed orange juice, water, pineapple-orange juice, and ginger in a large saucepan. Bring mixture to a boil. Remove from heat. Add tea bags; cover and steep 5 to 10 minutes. Discard tea bags. Strain mixture, discarding ginger and orange rind. Cover and chill. Serve over ice.

Serves 4

Nutritional Information per serving:
Calories: 90 • Fat: 0 • Protein: 1 gm.
Carb.: 21 gm. • Cholesterol: 0 • Fiber: very low

Minted Iced Tea Slush

Cold and refreshing.

2 cups water
6 tea bags, mint flavored
2 tablespoons sugar
1 cup orange juice

1 tablespoon lemon juice,
undiluted
3 cups club soda, chilled

Bring water to a boil. Pour over tea bags. Cover and let stand 5 minutes. Discard tea bags. Add sugar to taste. Add orange juice and lemon juice; stir well. Pour mixture into a baking pan. Cover and freeze 2 hours.

Spoon mixture into a pitcher. Stir in club soda. Stir gently until mixture becomes slushy, breaking up frozen pieces with a spoon.

Serves 6

Nutritional Information per serving:
Calories: 40 • Fat: 0 • Protein: 0
Carb.: 10 gm. • Cholesterol: 0 Fiber: very low

Peach Strawberry Swirl

Peachy smooth.

1 peach
1 cup fresh or frozen strawberries
1 medium banana

8 ounces low-fat vanilla yogurt
5 ice cubes (optional)

Combine all ingredients in food processor. Process until smooth.

Serves 3

Nutritional Information per serving:
Calories: 115 • Fat: 1 gm. • Protein: 5 gm.
Carb.: 22 gm. • Cholesterol: 5 mg. • Fiber: low

273

Strawberry Banana Pectin Smoothie

The fruit pectin adds fiber and smoothness.
This drink provides 3 grams of soluble fiber.

1 small banana, sliced
1/2 cup skim milk

1/3 cup frozen or fresh strawberries
2 tablespoons fruit pectin (Sure-Jell)

Place all ingredients in blender. Process until smooth. Serve immediately.

Serves 1

Nutritional Information per serving:
Calories: 220 • Fat: 0 • Protein: 5 gm.
Carb.: 50 gm. • Cholesterol: 2 mg. • Fiber: low

Strawberry Refresher

Tasty combination of fruit and yogurt.

1 cup strawberries
1/2 cup orange juice
2 tablespoons powdered sugar

8 ounces low-fat raspberry or
   lemon yogurt
5 ice cubes (optional)

Combine all ingredients in blender. Cover and process until smooth.

Serves 3

Nutritional Information per serving:
Calories: 100 • Fat: 1 gm. • Protein: 5 gm.
Carb.: 18 gm. • Cholesterol: 5 mg. • Fiber: low

274

Watermelon Slush

Watermelon is so special because it is
refreshing when your appetite is poor.

8 cups cubed, seeded watermelon
1/4 cup sifted powdered sugar

6 ounces frozen lemonade
   concentrate, thawed
mint sprigs (optional)

Place cubed watermelon in a large bowl. Cover and freeze.

Combine watermelon, sugar, and undiluted lemonade in food processor. Process until smooth. Garnish each serving with a sprig of mint.

Serves 6

Nutritional Information per serving:
Calories: 100 • Fat: 0 • Protein: 1 gm.
Carb.: 24 gm. • Cholesterol: 0 • Fiber: very low

Appendices

Dietary Supplement Selections

This is a listing of a few of the available supplements on the market. Formulations are continually changing. Read labels to make appropriate choices for you.

Product	Serving Size	Calories	Protein gm.	Fat gm.	Special Characteristics
Advera (Ross)	8 oz.	303	14.2	5.4	High calorie & protein
Boost (Mead Johnson)	8 oz.	240	10.0	4.0	High calorie & protein Low fat (4 gm)
Carnation Instant Breakfast	1 pkg. with 1 c. skim milk	220	12.0	1.0	High protein Low fat (1 gm)
Carnation Instant Breakfast	10 oz. can	200	12.0	3.0	Low fat (3 gm)
Choice-dm (Mead Johnson)	8 oz.	250	10.6	12.0	Balanced for diabetics (22 gm carbohydrates)
Deliver (Mead Johnson)	8 oz.	470	17.7	24.0	High calorie Mild, pleasant taste
Ensure (Ross)	8 oz.	250	9.0	9.0	Lactose/Milk free High protein
Ensure Plus	8 oz.	355	13.0	13.0	Lactose/Milk free High calorie & protein
Ensure High Protein	8 oz.	225	12.0	6.0	Lactose /Milk free High protein
Ensure Light	8 oz.	200	10.0	3.0	Lower calorie, Low fat
Ensure with Fiber	8 oz.	260	9.4	8.8	Lactose/Milk free High fiber
Equate (Wal-Mart)	8 oz.	250	9.0	9.0	Lower cost
Equate Plus	8 oz.	360	13.0	13.0	High calorie, Lower cost
Glucerna (Ross)	8 oz.	240	10.0	13.0	Balanced for diabetics (22 gm carbohydrates)

DIETARY SUPPLEMENT SELECTIONS

Product	Serving Size	Calories	Protein gm.	Fat gm.	Special Characteristics
Lipisorb (Mead Johnson)	8 oz.	240	8.4	11.5	85% of fat is MCT oil Marketed for patients with HIV and fat malabsorption
Magnacal (Sherwood)	8 oz.	500	17.5	20.0	Very high calorie Vanilla only
Meritene (Sandoz)	1 pkg. with 1 c. skim milk	200	18.0	0.0	High protein. Mix in a variety of foods
Nutra Start (Advanced Nut. Foods)	8 oz.	210	10.0	2.5	Low fat, Lactose-free
Osmolite (Ross)	8 oz.	250	8.8	9.0	Bland, plain flavor
Osmolite HN	8 oz.	250	10.5	9.0	High protein Bland, plain flavor
Resource (Sandoz)	8 oz.	250	8.8	8.8	Lactose/Milk free
Resource Plus	8 oz.	355	13.0	12.6	Lactose/Milk free High calorie & protein
Resource Fructose Sweetened	8 oz.	250	15.0	11.0	High calorie
Resource Fruit Beverage	8 oz.	180	8.8	0	Lactose/Milk free Clear liquid
Scandi Shakes (Scandipharm)	3 oz. powder with 1 c. whole milk	600	12.0	30.0	Very high calorie High protein & fat Lactose free available Great taste
Slim Fast-Ultra	11 oz.	200–220	7–10	1.5–3	Similar composition to Ensure Light
Sport Shake (Mid-Amer. Dairymen)	11 oz.	410	13.0	13.0	High calorie & protein
Sustacal (Mead Johnson)	8 oz.	240	8.8	8.0	Lactose/Milk free High protein
Sustacal Hi Pro	8 oz.	240	15.0	6.0	High protein
Sustacal with Fiber	8 oz.	250	10.8	8.0	Lactose/Milk free High fiber
Sustacal Plus	8 oz.	360	14.0	14.0	Lactose free High calorie & protein
Sweet Success (Nestle)	11 oz.	200	11.0	3.0	

DIETARY SUPPLEMENT SELECTIONS

Product	Serving Size	Calories	Protein gm.	Fat gm.	Special Characteristics
Walgreen's Nutritional Supplement	8 oz.	250	8.8	8.8	Low cost
Walgreen's Nutritional Supplement Plus	8 oz.	355	13.0	12.6	Low cost

There can be great variability in prices and in local availability. Products may be purchased in some pharmacies, drug stores, grocery stores, and discount department stores.

Modular components that can be added for extra calories:

Polycose or Sumacal 23 calories/Tbsp.

Lipomul 6 calories/cc (90 calories/Tbsp.)

MCT Oil 8 calories/cc (116 calories/Tbsp.)

Some products can be ordered directly from the companies and shipped to your home. Phone numbers:

Mead Johnson 1 (800) 247-7893

Nestle Foods 1 (800) 289-7313

Ross Labs 1 (800) 544-7495

Sandoz 1 (800) 446-6380

ScandiPharm 1 (800) 4 SCANDI (1[800] 472-2634)

High-Potassium Foods

Many medications deplete the body of potassium. To help counteract this effect, choose foods rich in potassium daily. (*denotes the lower-fiber choices)

Food	Serving Size	Mg. of Potassium
almonds	1/4 cup	225
artichoke	1 medium	315
avocado	1/2 fresh	600–900 depending on variety
banana	1 medium	450
beans, lima	1/2 cup	350
beans, navy	1/2 cup	300
beans, kidney	1/2 cup	350
cantaloupe*	1/4 medium	400
dried apricots	1/2 cup	635
dried dates	5 pitted	260
dried figs	5	650
dried prunes	5 large	300
dried raisins	1/2 cup	550
fish, flounder*	3 ounces	450
fish, halibut*	3 ounces	465
kiwifruit	1 medium	250
lentils	1/2 cup cooked	250
milk*	1 cup	375
orange	1 medium	260
orange juice*	3/4 cup	375
pineapple*	1/2 cup canned	125
pineapple juice*	3/4 cup	200
potato*	1 medium baked	780
prune juice	3/4 cup	450
pumpkin	1/2 cup	300
roast beef *	3 ounces	330
scallops*	3 ounces	365
sirloin steak*	3 ounces	300
split peas	1/2 cup cooked	300
squash, summer*	1/2 cup cooked	150
squash, winter (acorn, butternut, hubbard)	1/2 cup cooked	470

Food	Serving Size	Mg. of Potassium
sweet potato	1/2 cup canned	250
Swiss chard	1/2 cup cooked	485
tomato*	1 medium raw	300
tomatoes*	1/2 cup canned	260
tomato juice*	3/4 cup	400
yogurt, fruit flavored*	1 cup	440

Magnesium-Rich Foods

Some medications deplete the body of magnesium. To help counteract this effect, eat several servings of foods rich in magnesium each day.

Food	Serving Size	Mg. of Magnesium
apricots, dried	10 halves	16
fresh	3 medium	8
beans, red kidney	1/2 cup	45
white beans	1/2 cup	65
bread, white enriched	1 slice	4
whole wheat	1 slice	18
broccoli	1/2 cup cooked	18
cereals, All Bran	1 ounce	100
raisin bran	1 ounce	50
chickpeas	1/2 cup canned	35
chocolate candy	3 ounces	70–90
cocoa powder	1 Tbsp.	25
coconut, dried	1 ounce	25
corn	1/2 cup	35
figs, dried	1 fig	10
milk	1 cup	35
nuts, almonds	1/4 cup	100
Brazil nuts	1/4 cup	65
cashews	1/4 cup	85
peanuts	1/4 cup	50
pecans	1/4 cup	35
English walnuts	1/4 cup	150
rice, brown	1/2 cup	25
shrimp	3 ounces	30
spinach	1/2 cup cooked	70
	1/2 cup raw	20
wheat bran	1 ounce	130
wheat germ	1 ounce (3 Tbsp.)	100

Food and Nutrition Services, University of Wisconsin Hospital and Clinics

Index

281

283

INDEX

285

287